HIDDEN
SCOTLAND

The best of Edinburgh, curated by Hidden Scotland.

Camera Obscura Rooftop View

Welcome to Hidden Scotland's guide to Edinburgh, a city unlike any other. Scotland's capital fits all manner of descriptions – time capsule, trendsetter, visitor magnet, festival heartland – but above all it simply is what it is: a place apart. Topped by a fortress and stuffed with big sights and mazy stories, it successfully straddles the last millennium and a half by somehow being both locked in the past and fixated on the future.

As such, all life finds a place here. Some half a million souls call the city home year-round, but many times that number descend on its streets at different points in the calendar. From the rainbow-feathered cornucopia of the summer Fringe to the massed merry-making of Hogmanay – not to mention a whole galaxy of other concerts, exhibitions, parades and parties – this is somewhere that routinely feels like the place to be.

You're holding in your hands a key to the city. Over the following pages, you'll find a hand-picked assortment of different diversions to delve into. The range is suitably broad. There are monuments, cafés, theatres and galleries; walking routes, gift-buying tips, guided tours and whisky tastings; restaurants, picture houses, pubs and bookshops. Some of these attractions are well known while others fly under the radar. It's our sincere hope that you enjoy discovering them.

Edinburgh is nothing without context, of course, so there's ample space for historical tales, cultural highlights, suggested itineraries and the quirkier elements that give the city such a special reputation. And naturally, we've also included a fantastic range of hotels and out-of-town excursions.

Time spent here is generally time to relish, no matter what the season, and we hope this guide allows you to make the most of all Edinburgh has to offer.

Introduction

Things to Do

Food & Drink

Stories

134

Shops

Accommodation

156

Trips

172

Perth

Inverness

Aberdeen

Dundee

Stirling

Edinburgh

Glasgow

Approximate travel time by road:

Aberdeen	2 hrs 35 mins	Inverness	3 hrs 10 mins	Perth	1 hr 5 mins
Dundee	1 hr 30 mins	Stirling	1 hr 0 mins	Glasgow	1 hr 10 mins

Edinburgh

Waverley Bridge

History hangs on Edinburgh like a cloak. Even on a gloomy day, Scotland's national capital can feel like something from a gilt-edged storybook. It's a city of taverns and tenements, of steep cobbled streets and ancient hills, of grand townhouses and age-old churches. The whole destination is at once real and unreal: tour guides patrol the pavements just as ghosts flitter in the shadows. That the whole urban scene is topped by a mighty, cliff-perched castle – complete with endless tales of its own – seems only fitting.

Best-selling local author Alexander McCall Smith called it "a city of shifting light, of changing skies, of sudden vistas – a city so beautiful it breaks the heart again and again". But Edinburgh is no mere museum piece. To the half a million or so people who call it home, this is a place of energy and hard graft, a living, sleepless metropolis with a thousand-sided personality and serious culinary and creative pedigree.

The sloping Royal Mile – with the castle at its top and the Palace of Holyroodhouse at its bottom – is the most obvious focal point, but be sure to spread your gaze elsewhere. The city as a whole is almost brimming over with quality galleries, restaurants, pubs, museums and other diversions. For many visitors, of course, the city is also synonymous with its extraordinary summer festivals – most notably the all-conquering Fringe – when the streets and theatres fizz with crowds and performers.

This pairing of the historic and the dynamic – medieval bulwarks on one hand, cutting-edge arts on the other – is one of the main reasons why the population can at times treble with the influx of visitors. Other cities might have big-name sights, hard-held traditions and world-famous events, but nowhere packages them up in quite the same way as Edinburgh. The pull is perhaps best summed up by a quote from city-born artist Richard DeMarco, a tireless champion of the visual and performing arts. "The Scots think of it as their capital", he has said. "They're too possessive. Edinburgh belongs to the world."

History

Castle Rock represents more than just a great social media snap. It's the stronghold around which the city grew, with excavations revealing human habitation on the clifftop as far back as 900 BC.

In the early years of the first millennium AD, advancing Roman legions found Castle Rock fortified by a tribe of ancient Britons, the Votadini. Some time later, another tribe – the Gododdin – erected a fort here known as Din Eidyn. When the Angles—essentially the English— invaded in the 7th century, they named it Eidyn Burh, with 'burh' meaning fort. The Scots eventually recaptured it, leading to centuries of expansion and shifting power.

By the time of James III's reign in the 15th century, the city was already thriving as a medieval centre of trade and activity, becoming the official capital of Scotland in 1452. Its prestige was only heightened when the gardens and Georgian buildings of the 'New Town' appeared towards the end of the 18th century. Today, with Castle Rock still at its heart, Edinburgh's star shines no less brightly.

Vennel Steps

LEITH

Areas

Edinburgh is a place that isn't easily contained by the frameworks of a neighbourhood map, with districts that have a tendency to spill into and across each other. Among it all, however, there's a sense of geographical order, and this guidebook has curated the best of the city across six key areas.

OLD TOWN

NEW TOWN

STOCKBRIDGE

For what is essentially a melee of buildings on an extinct volcano, Edinburgh's Old Town packs in an astonishing amount of appeal. The lanes, cobbles and tenements hold history and eccentricity at every turn, and its sloping centrepiece – the Royal Mile – is topped and tailed by the Palace of Holyroodhouse at the bottom and the castle at the top.

Despite its name – accurate about two centuries ago – the New Town was mainly built between the 1760s and the 1850s, ostensibly to give wealthier residents somewhere more salubrious to live than the cramped and rickety Old Town. It was laid out on a grand scale, and its tall townhouses, open squares and wide thoroughfares are still evident today.

Overlapping the northern edge of the New Town, Stockbridge is an attractive quarter featuring terraced townhouses with the Water of Leith flowing right through the neighbourhood. The Royal Botanic Garden is its biggest draw – certainly in terms of area – but you'll find any number of great spots to dine, drink and soak up the local culture.

SOUTHSIDE

WEST END

LEITH

This greener, more relaxed side to the city is spread out south of the Old Town. Its location gives it strong university links – which in turn means no shortage of places to eat, relax, and unwind – and the presence of The Meadows, one of Edinburgh's best outdoor spaces, is a further boon.

Lying directly to the west of the New Town, this is another central district brimming with arty venues, indie stores and Georgian terraces. It's undeniably one of the most affluent parts of the city, a fact that translates into some superb places for visitors to shop, stay and spend time.

Once a major trading port, then a rundown dockland district, Leith's reinvention has seen it recently named as one of the coolest neighbourhoods not just in Scotland, but the world. Judge for yourself by paying a visit to the Shore and its surrounds – you'd be wise to set aside plenty of time for eating and drinking.

How to use this guide

This guide works in two ways. On one-level it's a traditional guidebook, an item to live in your pocket or backpack, a compendium to bookmark and make notes in. But there's more..

On the listings pages you'll find QR codes, which when scanned will take you to a Hidden Scotland webpage. For extra information on any of the listings, simply enter the relevant listing number on this webpage. It's that simple.

And that's not all. The city stories in this guide also have their own QR codes. Scan them and you'll be given the option to hear each tale being narrated.

Scan here for more information on each listing. Enter the listing number to see our digital map, images and additional inspiration.

Upper Bow Street, Old Town

A city for all seasons

There's no bad time to visit the Scottish capital. Some months, however, are busier than others. Edinburgh has a packed annual programme of festivals, concerts and events, but finding accommodation can be a challenge in the summer and hotels tend to hike up their prices - so don't rock up in August without booking somewhere to stay.

The big hitters are Hogmanay - the city's legendary New Year celebrations - and of course the International Festival and Edinburgh Fringe in August, but there's also a strong supporting cast of events throughout the year.

Mar	Edinburgh Science Festival sciencefestival.co.uk
Apr	Beltane Fire Festival beltane.org
May	Edinburgh International Children's Festival imaginate.org.uk
	Edinburgh Tradfest edinburghtradfest.com
Jun	Meadows Festival meadowsfestival.co.uk
	Hidden Door Festival hiddendoorarts.org
	Leith Festival leithfestival.com
Jul	Edinburgh Jazz & Blues Festival edinburghjazzfestival.com
	Edinburgh Food Festival edfoodfest.com
	Edinburgh International Festival eif.co.uk

Aug	Edinburgh Fringe Festival edfringe.com
	Edinburgh Art Festival edinburghartfestival.com
	Edinburgh International Book Festival edbookfest.co.uk
	Edinburgh International Film Festival edfilmfest.org.uk
	The Royal Edinburgh Military Tattoo edintattoo.co.uk
	Edinburgh Foodies Festival foodiesfestival.com
Oct	Scottish International Storytelling Festival sisf.org.uk
	Samhuinn Fire Festival beltane.org
Dec	Edinburgh's Winter Festival edwinterfest.com
	Hogmanay edinburghshogmanay.com

Getting around

TOUCHDOWN

Edinburgh Airport is to the west of the city, around eight miles from the city centre; the journey takes about half an hour by taxi.

There are also good public transport links. Airlink Buses depart every ten minutes from the airport to the centre with drop-off points at Haymarket train station in the West End and Waverley train station just off Princes Street in between the Old Town and the New Town.

Trams also depart from outside the main terminal into the New Town every seven minutes between 7am and 7pm and every 15 minutes outside peak times.

The main bus station is in the New Town on Elder Street in between St Andrew Square and the St James Quarter.

ROUTE MAP

Getting around Edinburgh is relatively easy. It's a compact - if hilly and cobbled - city and walking is a good way to explore, dipping into little alleys and wynds, zigzagging across its leafy parks, curving round the elegant Georgian crescents.

Tip: Pack your trainers!

Buses and Trams

There is a good public transport network of buses and trams if you want to venture further to neighbourhoods such as Portobello or Leith. Buy a day ticket valid on Lothian buses and trams if you're going to be hopping on and off.

Tip: You need exact change to buy a single ticket on the bus.

Cycling

Although many of Edinburgh's streets are cobbled there's a good network of off-road cycle paths around the city. And if you're worried about the hills, most rental companies offer e-bikes alongside road and hybrid bikes.

Tip: The Tartan Bicycle Company and Cycle Scotland also offer self-guided, guided and bespoke bike tours.

Tartan Bicycle Company
tartanbiketours.co.uk

Leith Cycle Co
leithcycleco.com

Cycle Scotland
cyclescotland.co.uk

Park and Ride

There are seven park and rides spread around the city. Six are directly on the outskirts: Ingliston and Hermiston to the west, Sheriffhall and Straiton to the south and Wallyford and Newcraighall to the east. The seventh, Ferrytoll, is to the north across the Forth Bridge. All offer regular, prompt access into the city.

Parking

Most hotels don't have car parks. Some, such as The Balmoral, offer valet parking. The Malmaison in Leith has a large free car park. Edinburgh Council website lists multi storey car parks around the city: edinburgh.gov.uk

Tip: Central area street parking is charged until 6.30pm (8.30am start) Monday to Saturday, and until 6.30pm (12.30pm start) on Sunday. Elsewhere, charges apply until 5.30pm, Monday to Friday. Free outside these hours.

Electric Vehicle Charging points

There are charging points around the city, visit ChargePlace Scotland's site chargeplacescotland.org

Victoria Street

More than four million visitors a year can't be wrong. With history around every corner and a restless spirit of cultural innovation, this is a fast-moving – and photogenic – city, where the main challenge is fitting everything in.

Things to Do

Dean Village

Walks, Wildlife & Nature

They had their heads screwed on, those early civic planners. Edinburgh might be a compact city, but it packs in plenty of greenery, gardens and open spaces, helped by the presence of its famous seven hills.

Dunbar's Close
Old Town

Snaffled away off the Royal Mile you'll find this charming little garden, with handsome trees, neatly partitioned beds and several benches for the foot-weary. It's a princely picnic spot, and improbably close to the throng.

 Physic Garden, Palace of Holyroodhouse
Old Town

The palace's original physic garden was founded in 1670 and evolved to become the Royal Botanic Garden, but a far newer version was opened in 2020, with three different zones representing different stages of history.

 James Hutton Memorial Garden
Old Town

Recognised as the father of modern geology, 18th-century scientist James Hutton is remembered in this small Old Town garden, which stands where his house was once located.

 Moray House Garden
Old Town

Much famed as an urban oasis when it was planted and laid out in the 17th century, this Old Town garden is now a fraction of its former self but remains an interesting diversion. Remarkably, the humble summerhouse that still stands is said to be where Scottish and English representatives signed the Act of Union in 1707.

 Princes Street Gardens
New Town

Are these the UK's most panoramic public gardens? Quite possibly. Made up of two neighbouring parks and dating back to the building of the New Town, the centrally located Princes Street Gardens grant superb castle views. They're also dotted with all manner of points of interest of their own, from the towering dark spire of the Scott Monument to an animal statue commemorating Wojtek, the so-called "soldier bear".

 Scan here for more information on each listing. Enter the listing number to see our digital map, images and additional inspiration.

View from Calton Hill

 Archivist's Garden
New Town

This courtyard garden contains close to 60 different species and was created to celebrate the link between certain plants and "Scotland's collective memory". As such, you'll find everything from sea thrift and myrtle to heather and iris, with due reverence also given to the thistle – part of Scottish heraldry since 1488.

 Calton Hill
New Town

Any walk to the summit of this UNESCO-listed hill is a walk to remember. Topped by numerous monuments and some strikingly neo-classical architecture (said to have been the main factor behind Edinburgh's "Athens of the North" nickname), it also boasts frankly spectacular views over the rest of the city.

Circus Lane

Royal Botanic Garden
Stockbridge

A world-class botanic garden in 72 acres of grounds, with giant redwoods, rhododendrons, Alpine houses and a famed rock garden among the features to show for its three and a half centuries of history.

 Circus Lane
Stockbridge

A curving vision of greenery and cobbles – and big on Instagram – this charming residential street was originally lined with stables. It's close to St Stephen Street in the Stockbridge area.

DID YOU KNOW?

Where the peaceful Princes Street Gardens are today, there used to be the Nor' Loch. Created in 1460 as a city defense, it unfortunately turned foul due to sewage from the Royal Mile above. This once strategic water body became a nuisance before transforming into the beautiful gardens we see now.

 Dean Village
Stockbridge

Huddled around the Water of Leith, near the Stockbridge area, you'll find this atmospheric collection of 19th-century buildings and old houses. Its most famous feature, Well Court, was used as accommodation for the workers at the watermills.

 Inverleith Park
Stockbridge

"The city is to be congratulated on the acquisition and opening of this magnificent park which... will form in all time coming... an open space of unrivalled beauty." So said Cockburn Council of Inverleith Park in 1891, and more than 130 years later the 54-acre park remains a gem, complete with swans, wildflowers, a boating pond, wetlands and tennis courts. It's right next to the Royal Botanic Garden.

Walks, Wildlife & Nature

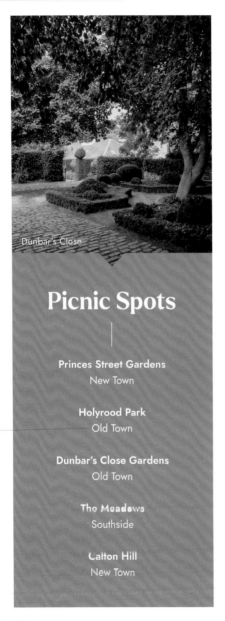

Dunbar's Close

Picnic Spots

Princes Street Gardens
New Town

Holyrood Park
Old Town

Dunbar's Close Gardens
Old Town

The Meadows
Southside

Calton Hill
New Town

 Duddingston Loch
Southside

A natural freshwater loch within walking distance of the Royal Mile? You'd better believe it. Duddingston Loch provides a blast of natural wilderness in the confines of the city. Surrounded by reedbeds and woodland, it serves as a fine habitat for herons and wintering wildfowl, and otters have even been spotted.

 Dr Neil's Garden
Southside

A fine option for a break from the crowds. Set up in the 1960s by Drs Andrew and Nancy Neil, this free-to-enter garden is a landscaped oasis at the foot of Arthur's Seat, on the edge of Duddingston Loch. Combining evergreens and heathers with alpine plants and all manner of seasonal flowers, it creates a tangible sense of calm.

 Craigmillar Castle Park
Southside

Woodland trails, a converted farmhouse and an age-old castle – once a haven for Mary Queen of Scots – provide the setting for this unique swathe of green, lying south of where the city walls once stretched. Pheasants, squirrels and even deer still call it home.

Arthur's Seat
Southside

Towering 251 metres above sea level, the iconic volcanic peak of Arthur's Seat offers a proper hill walk close to the heart of Edinburgh. Urban hikes don't come much better. One theory is that the name was originally Àrd-na-Said, which loosely translates as "Height of Arrows".

Braid Hills
Southside

A rolling belt of open land to the southwest of the city, the Braid Hills are famous not just for the sweeping views back across to the Firth of Forth but for being home to a historic golf course.

Arthur's Seat

George Square Garden
Southside

Close to The Meadows is this leafy city square, laid out in (you guessed it) the Georgian era and long a popular venue for Fringe performances. Arthur Conan Doyle and Sir Walter Scott are among those to have lived in the surrounding houses.

The Meadows
Southside

South of the Old Town is this large expanse of grassland, criss-crossed by tree-lined paths and offering green respite from the hullabaloo of the city centre. It's well worth visiting in April, when its spectacular cherry blossom display heralds the onset of spring.

Scan here for more information on each listing. Enter the listing number to see our digital map, images and additional inspiration.

Walks, Wildlife & Nature

Harbourside Leith

19 **Water of Leith Walkway**
Leith

This 13-mile riverside walkway runs next to or close to the Water of Leith for almost its entire length, giving a simple way of stepping away from the hubbub of the streets. The northern end of the path is in Leith itself, while the southern end is way out in the foothills of the Pentland range. As such, it winds past all sorts of cultural, natural and historical points of interest – from the Royal Botanic Garden and Murrayfield Stadium to the Scottish Gallery of Modern Art.

20 **Harbourside Leith**
Leith

The harbourside stretch known as The Shore is where you'll see the most evidence of Leith's long history, with cobbled quays and age-old maritime buildings – but a stroll also gives you the chance to enjoy its more modern charms, with some brilliant places to stop and refuel. And if you're after something really special? Three Michelin-starred restaurants – Heron, Restaurant Martin Wishart and The Kitchin are clustered in the vicinity.

Susan

Lifestory

New Town

See page 140 for more information on Lifestory.

How would you spend a rainy day in the city?

Edinburgh is blessed with some of the finest galleries you'll ever visit. From The Portrait Gallery just up the road from us, to smaller spaces like &Gallery and The Ingleby Gallery which feature diverse artists and frequently changing exhibitions. Follow that up with a coffee or matcha at The Milkman and watch the world go by.

Where is your go to coffee shop in the area?

Our neighbourhood has great independent cafés like Fortitude, Artisan Roast and Bearded Baker. Recently, the owners of Spry Wine opened a gorgeous café called Ante in the unit underneath, which adds something new to our area, its interior and menu reflects a considered, minimal aesthetic which we love!

MUST SEE IN YOUR NEIGHBOURHOOD?

Calton Hill

The Ingleby Gallery

Royal Botanic Gardens

Lannan Bakery

The Gardener's Lodge

Unusual & Interesting

A city this multifarious is always going to have its quirks – and Edinburgh boasts peculiarities by the barrel-load. From "murder dolls" to a stuffed sheep, its oddities are as fascinating as they are diverse.

Burke and Hare Murder Dolls

 21

Burke and Hare Murder Dolls
Old Town

The National Museum of Scotland has no shortage of remarkable exhibits, but few are as strange as this set of tiny dolls in coffins, reportedly found in parkland by two young boys in the 1830s. The overriding theory is that they were created a decade earlier by notorious murderers Burke and Hare, to represent their real-life victims.

DID YOU KNOW?

Edinburgh's Greyfriars Kirkyard features Iron Mortsafes, devised around 1816 to deter grave robbers, to protect bodies from being stolen for the purposes of medical science.

The Witches Well
Old Town

This is not your average memorial. On a wall close to Edinburgh Castle is fixed an old drinking fountain – it's easy to miss but tells a poignant story. It was erected in the 1890s to honour the numberless unfortunates who were burned at the stake for "witchcraft" between the 15th and 18th centuries, many of them close to where the memorial now stands.

Greyfriars Kirkyard Graves
Old Town

If some of the surnames on the graves of Greyfriars Kirkyard seem familiar – Potter, McGonagall, Scrimgeour, Black – there's a reason. JK Rowling is thought to have taken inspiration from some of the tombstones here when naming her characters. Look out for the resting place of Thomas Riddell – the original Tom Riddle.

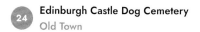
Edinburgh Castle Dog Cemetery
Old Town

Scamp, Dobbler, Yum Yum and Tinker are among the four-legged friends laid to rest in this small burial plot in the grounds of the castle, used since Queen Victoria's reign as a burial site for regimental dogs.

World's End Close
Old Town

This plaque on the Royal Mile, marking a tight passageway, signifies the spot where travellers and residents were once forced to pay a toll to leave or enter the city. For those locals of limited means – of which, sadly, there were plenty – it meant they were effectively confined to Edinburgh for life, hence the name of the close.

Dolly the Sheep
Old Town

One of the National Museum of Scotland's most popular exhibits is a stuffed ewe. This is, of course, the now-legendary Dolly the Sheep, who became a scientific phenomenon in the 1990s as the first mammal to be cloned from an adult cell.

Camera Obscura and World of Illusions
Old Town

Edinburgh's mind-bending Camera Obscura – which uses prisms to beam a live view of the city onto a concave viewing surface – dates back to the 1850s. It's a remarkable attraction, now paired with several floors worth of other illusions.

Unusual & Interesting

Golden Hawk Sculpture at Gladstone's Land

Old Town

Gleaming on the side of an old tenement in the Old Town, this eye-catching golden raptor provides an avian dazzle against the ageing stones of the building, its wings outstretched as though bound for some distant eyrie.

Susannah Alice Stephen Memorial

Old Town

Hidden off the Royal Mile, this unusual statue features a parakeet in a garden trug, and was commissioned by the friends of landscape designer "Zannah" Morris after her death in a diving accident in 1997. A great lover of life, it's said she was also fond of the closes tucked away around the Old Town.

Morocco's Land Effigy

Old Town

Two storeys high on an old wall along the Canongate you'll spot an unusual-looking statue. Dressed in North African robes and sporting a voluminous headdress, it's said to have been created in homage to the emperor of Morocco in the 1600s.

David Hume Statue

Old Town

It's not every day you see a man in a toga with shiny toes. This statue of David Hume, near the top of the Royal Mile, portrays the famous philosopher as an ancient Greek – and rubbing his toes is said to bring wisdom to passers-by.

The Heave Away House

Old Town

The inscription above the entrance to Paisley Close – "Heave awa' chaps, I'm no' dead yet", accompanied by the engraving of a boy's head – commemorates the sole survivor of a seven-storey tenement collapse on the same spot in 1861. More than 30 people died, but a voice from the rubble meant rescue attempts weren't completely futile.

DID YOU KNOW?

When Robert the Bruce destroyed Edinburgh Castle, he respected St Margaret so much that he left her chapel standing. It's now the oldest intact building in the city.

The Ivy Heart of Chessels Court

The Heart of Midlothian
Old Town

Don't be alarmed if you see locals spitting on the Royal Mile. The Heart of Midlothian is a heart-shaped mosaic built into the cobbles outside St Giles' Cathedral – it marks the entrance to what was once the Old Tolbooth, a jail renowned for its grisly treatment of inmates. Spitting on the heart has since become a form of good luck, as well as a way of showing disdain for the executions that took place here.

The Ivy Heart of Chessels Court
Old Town

Looking for an uncrowded spot for that perfect Old Town Instagram post? If the answer's yes, head to Chessels Court off the Royal Mile, where you'll spot an ivy-covered wall, its leaves trimmed into the shape of a large heart. And if the answer's no – hey, we can't all be social media-savvy – just enjoy the find.

Gilbert the Phone Box

Wojtek the Soldier Bear Memorial

35 **Gilbert the Phone Box**
New Town

36 **Wojtek the Soldier Bear Memorial**
New Town

Standing outside Stewart Christie and Co's tailor shop on Queen Street is a classic red phone box, nicknamed "Gilbert" and reinvented as a debonair photo booth complete with hats, books and a vintage phone. Pop into the shop to ask for the key – you'll be asked to make a small donation to Save The Children.

The unlikely story of a bear named Wojtek – who began his life being purchased as a cub by the roadside in Iran, went on to serve in the Polish army (yes, really), and spent his dotage in Edinburgh Zoo – has been immortalised by a statue in Princes Street Gardens.

Scan here for more information on each listing. Enter the listing number to see our digital map, images and additional inspiration.

Library of Mistakes
New Town

Recent British history suggests that this West End business and finance library is aptly named. It's a charitable venture and aims to promote the study of financial history – as well as the ability to learn lessons from past errors.

Abraham Lincoln Statue
New Town

A Calton Hill cemetery might not be the most obvious place to find a statue of the 16th president of the USA, but there's a good reason why it's here. Old Calton Burial Ground includes a memorial devoted to Scots who fought and died in the American Civil War. It's topped by a statue of Lincoln – the only example of its kind in Scotland.

The Gardener's Lodge
New Town

The pretty red-brick cottage in Princes Street Gardens was originally home to the head gardener. Today it remains an unlikely sight in the heart of the city, a bucolic little house ringed by rosebushes. It also featured in the CBeebies series Teacup Travels, as the cottage of Great Aunt Lizzie.

Lighthouse Model at 84 George Street
New Town

Among the classy shops and elegant townhouses of George Street, you'll notice a model lighthouse erected outside the first-floor window of the Northern Lighthouse Board building. It's right above the doorway.

Ross Fountain
New Town

Purchased at London's 1862 Great Exhibition by an Edinburgh gunmaker named Daniel Ross, this 19th-century cast-iron fountain now provides a highly decorative focal point in Princes Street Gardens.

DID YOU KNOW?

The first municipal fire brigade in the world was formed in the city after the Great Fire of Edinburgh of 1824.

Scottish Poetry Library

Edinburgh Book Sculptures

Between March and November 2011, a series of meticulously crafted "sculptures" appeared around Edinburgh. Constructed from old books by an anonymous artist, they were intended as gifts to the city and its cultural institutions. Eleven of the sculptures can still be seen and admired — you'll find a map on the Scottish Poetry Library website.

 42 The Wild West in Springvalley Gardens
Southside

When the now-defunct South West Furniture Company struck on the idea of creating a mock Wild West scene off a Morningside side street in the mid-90s, they were inadvertently creating one of the city's stranger sights. Decades later, you'll still find a faded facade of dusty, one-horse-town buildings including signage for a cantina and a blacksmiths.

 43 Gilmerton Cove
Southside

There's more to the outlying Edinburgh suburb of Gilmerton than meets the eye. A set of hand-carved sandstone tunnels and chambers snake under the streets of this one-time mining village, and can be visited by appointment.

 44 Liberton Tower
Southside

This solid hilltop tower, on the southern outskirts of the city, now provides a holiday home with a difference. The four-storey building was first built in the 1450s and – after an ignoble period as a farm store and piggery – has since been restored to its former glory.

The Wild West in Springvalley Gardens

 Innocent Railway Tunnel
Southside

 Bore Stane
Southside

When the Edinburgh and Dalkeith Railway was constructed in the 1830s, to carry coal from the pits to the city, it soon earned the nickname the Innocent Railway – the most likely reason being because it was largely horse-drawn rather than powered by steam engines. Its most striking feature was a 518m long tunnel (the first railway tunnel in Scotland), which remains in situ and is still used regularly today by cyclists and walkers.

Along Morningside Road, on the boundary wall of the parish church, stands a weathered slab of stone. This is no ordinary lump of rock – the plaque below states that the Scottish standard was planted in it when troops were being readied at the Battle of Flodden in 1513. Retrieved from a field centuries later, it's been part of the wall here since 1852.

Unusual & Interesting

Riddle's Court

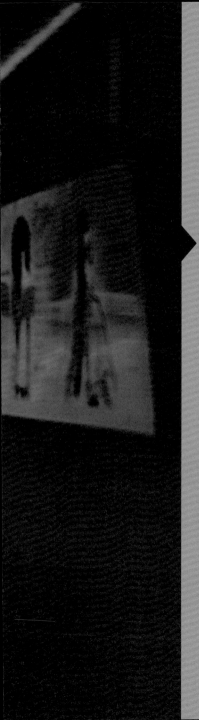

History & Museums

Edinburgh can often feel like a
city where the past is visible at
every turn, so delving into its
chief historical attractions is a
major part of understanding
what makes it tick.

Riddle's Court
Old Town

For an immersive look inside a grand tenement building, this Category A-listed attraction is hard to beat. The former merchant's house has been refurbished to the tune of £6 million, resulting in an interior full of panelling, paintings and other period details.

Surgeons' Hall Museums
Old Town

Reopened in 2015, the museums hold a gruesomely compelling collection of "natural and artificial curiosities" from the world of surgical pathology, including human remains and medical instruments. The complex is entered via an attractive garden.

The Flodden Wall and The Vennel Steps
Old Town

Part of the city's boundary defences in the 1560s, the crenellated remains of Flodden Wall still stand strong, close to where the so-called Vennel Steps give arguably the best – and some of the closest – castle views in the city.

The Writers' Museum
Old Town

Literary titans don't come much bigger than Robert Louis Stevenson, Sir Walter Scott and Robert Burns and this deservedly popular museum celebrates the lives and works of all three.

Greyfriars Kirkyard
Old Town

One of Edinburgh's more unlikely historical heroes is Greyfriars Bobby, the little Skye terrier who reportedly spent the last 14 years of his life sitting patiently by his late owner's grave. Bobby's statue now sits atop a granite fountain on the corner of George IV Bridge and Candlemaker Row, close to Greyfriars Kirkyard, the cemetery where he's now buried near his master.

Scotsman Steps
Old Town

Leading between Waverley Station's Market Street entrance and North Bridge, these 104 steps were reworked in 2010 by Turner Prize-winning artist Martin Creed, who formed each one of the stairs from a different type of marble.

The Writers' Museum

Greyfriars Bobby

 **Edinburgh Castle**
Old Town

Set aside several hours for a trip to the biggest ticket in town. Much of what you see today dates from the 18th and 19th centuries, when the complex evolved from a monarch's retreat to a garrison fortress. There's much to explore on a visit, including the hammer-beamed Great Hall, the tiny St Margaret's Chapel, the giant Mons Meg cannon and the glittering crown jewels known as the Honours of Scotland. The castle's famed One O'Clock Gun is still fired each day at the requisite hour – be warned that it's loud.

National Museum of Scotland

54 The Scottish Parliament Building
Old Town

An eye-catching vision of steel, oak and granite, the Scottish Parliament Building sits at the bottom of the Royal Mile. It was designed by Barcelona architect Enric Miralles and formally opened in 2004.

55 Palace of Holyroodhouse
Old Town

Still an official royal residence, and previously frequented by everyone from Mary Queen of Scots to Queen Elizabeth II – even Bonnie Prince Charlie reportedly used the Great Gallery for opulent evening balls – the lavish Palace of Holyroodhouse makes for an absorbing place to visit.

56 Magdalen Chapel
Old Town

Built in the 1540s – and therefore Edinburgh's last pre-Reformation Catholic chapel – this gem of a chapel on Cowgate is notable for lively historical details such as its age-old stained glass windows.

57 National Museum of Scotland
Old Town

A colossus of a museum charting the long story of the nation, touching on everything from prehistoric geology and the ups and downs of Scotland's medieval history to the developments of the 21st century. Art, design, science and tech all get a look in, while the building itself is a remarkable sight in its own right, centred on the cavernous atrium of the Grand Gallery.

58 St Giles' Cathedral
Old Town

A working church for almost exactly nine centuries (King David I founded it in 1124), and boasting a plum location halfway up the Royal Mile, St Giles' has a long and eventful past. It was John Knox's parish church during the Reformation, and in 1633 was made the cathedral of the newly formed Diocese of Edinburgh, by King Charles I.

TIP

When at St Giles' Cathedral, take time to visit the Thistle chapel which is hidden away in the back right corner of the cathedral.

History & Museums

Mercat Cross
Old Town

A Royal Mile landmark standing just outside St Giles' Cathedral, the Mercat (or Market) Cross has origins dating back almost seven centuries, although the current version – bearing royal arms and Latin inscriptions – was erected in the Victorian era.

 Lady Stair's Close
Old Town

There are more than 80 closes off the Royal Mile, but few are as picturesque – or as well-known – as this moody little courtyard, reached by a dark passageway and dominated by a 17th-century townhouse, once the home of the first Countess of Stair.

 Advocate's Close
Old Town

Leading off the Royal Mile, this narrow, 500-year-old close is notable among other things for the fine views it affords over the Scott Monument and Princes Street. It's named in honour of Sir James Stewart, a former Lord Advocate of Scotland in the early 18th century.

 Bakehouse Close
Old Town

Fans of historical drama Outlander might recognise this courtyard from several key scenes – on screen, Alexander Malcolm's print shop is based here, and it's also where Jamie is reunited with Claire – but the close's real-life past is rather more salacious, as a notorious red-light area.

 The People's Story Museum
Old Town

Housed in the former Canongate Tolbooth on the Royal Mile, this absorbing museum focuses on the stories of Edinburgh's working-class population from the 18th century to the modern day. Various tableaux from the past are recreated, including a war-era kitchen and a bookbinder's workshop.

 Museum of Edinburgh
Old Town

The bowl and collar of Greyfriars Bobby and a handsome collection of longcase clocks are among the exhibits at this museum on the Royal Mile. It's located in a former slum building and gives a colourful look at the city's past.

White Horse Close

 66 Museum on the Mound
Old Town

Money, money, money. This museum, which is indeed on the Mound, sits in what was once the head office of the Bank of Scotland. It takes a look at money and finance in all its forms – and, perhaps ironically, it's free.

 67 The Stones of Scotland
Old Town

Edinburgh's very own stone circle may not be ancient, but it has powerful symbolism nonetheless – the 32 stones that make up its perimeter come from each of the councils of Scotland. The sculpture, on Regent Park Road, was put in place in 2002.

 65 White Horse Close
Old Town

The origins of the name might remain something of a puzzle (one almost certainly apocryphal tale states that Mary Queen of Scots' mare was stabbed here) but there's no doubting the historical beauty of this courtyard off the Canongate, where a cluster of old buildings stand cheek by jowl over the flagstones.

 68 Gladstone's Land
Old Town

Sitting on the Royal Mile for more than four centuries, this high-tenement house has witnessed the comings and goings of countless traders, rogues and other Edinburgh characters. It's now an immersive visitor attraction, with guided tours giving insight into the building's story-rich past.

History & Museums

Walter Scott Monument

70 The Georgian House
New Town

You know what you're getting with this does-what-it-says-on-the-tin iconic New Town attraction – but it's still mightily impressive. Expect grand artworks, architectural pomp and intricate period furniture.

71 Dundas House
New Town

This imposing 18th-century townhouse was built for one of the wealthiest men in Scotland, businessman (and, regrettably, enabler of the slave trade) Sir Lawrence Dundas. These days it's a branch of the Royal Bank of Scotland, and can be visited by all.

69 Walter Scott Monument
New Town

Reaching a height of more than 60 metres, this Victorian Gothic totem of richly decorated sandstone features spiral staircases and almost seventy different statues, most notably Scott himself, who sits in marbled splendour in the centre space next to his dog Maida. The design was one of many submitted to a public competition in the 1830s. Given that the whole structure is essentially a tribute to a novelist, it's a remarkable sight.

DID YOU KNOW?

George IV's short kilt during his 1822 Scotland visit, orchestrated by Sir Walter Scott, became a pivotal moment in establishing the tartan as Scotland's national dress.

Dundas House

 Stockbridge Colonies
Stockbridge

Just to the south of the Royal Botanic Garden you'll find a remarkable piece of living history. The Stockbridge Colonies are made up of rows of terraced stone houses, constructed in the 19th century when the Industrial Revolution saw the city's population boom. These split-level Victorian workers' cottages are designed in a remarkable way, with the upper and lower apartments of each terrace accessed from different streets.

 Warriston Cemetery
Stockbridge

Tens of thousands of graves have been erected in this atmospheric, wildlife-rich cemetery since it was designed by architect David Cousins in the 1840s. Now sloping across 40 acres, it's the final resting place of several notable characters, including physician Sir James Young Simpson.

Leith Shore

 Leith Shore
Leith

 **The Signal Tower**
Leith

The Shore in Leith boasts a long maritime history, dating back to the Anglo-Saxon era. It has played host to monarchs like Mary Queen of Scots and George IV and saw critical events like the 1544 Rough Wooing. Pioneering in urban illumination, it introduced oil lamps in 1771 and electric lighting in 1895.

One of the most eye-catching buildings on the harbourside at Leith is this bulky, cylindrical tower, originally built as a windmill before being converted into a signal tower – a kind of beacon from which to send fire or smoke signals – in 1805. A ring of battlements adds to the drama.

 Scan here for more information on each listing. Enter the listing number to see our digital map, images and additional inspiration.

Rosanna
101 Bakery

Southside

See page 127 for more information on 101 Bakery.

What's the most popular sweet treat in the bakery?

Our cinnamon buns are probably our most popular treat! I developed the recipe before I opened the shop and they are accidentally vegan which makes them super light and fluffy. My absolute favourite however is our salted chocolate chip cookies. To me they are the perfect cookie, chewy, fudgy, salty and sweet.

Where would you take a friend visiting Edinburgh for the first time?

The Grassmarket for a gelato at Mary's Milk Bar, wander up to Hey Palu for a cocktail, lunch at the Palmerston followed by a stroll through Dean Village then down to the Shore. Razzo for pizza at dinner followed by drinks at Nauticus. On Sunday evening, we would listen to jazz at Malt and Hops.

MUST SEE IN YOUR NEIGHBOURHOOD?

Arthur's Seat

The Meadows

Cult Espresso

Noodles and Dumplings

The Royal Yacht Britannia

Activities

A city as visitor-friendly as Edinburgh has no shortage of different activities with which to occupy your time. Here are some of the best of them.

The Real Mary King's Close

76

The Real Mary King's Close
Old Town

There's plenty to enjoy – some of it gruesome, all of it gripping – on a one-hour guided tour of this historic close off the Royal Mile. The tours are led by costumed characters, and the experience has achieved enough renown to earn a five-star historic attraction rating from the Scottish Tourist Board.

It does a great job of delving into the real lives of the tenants who lived here over the centuries, using historical records to bring to life some of its characters such

as a household maid, a poet and a 'foul clenger', whose job it was to clean the houses of plague victims.

Mary King herself, who lends her name to the close, lived here in the 17th century and was a merchant burgess who sold cloth to keep her family supported. It transpires, however, that she also had a liking for fine wines and expensive ceramics, proving that, as is so often the case in Edinburgh, there's more to the past than meets the eye.

Blair Street Underground Vaults
Old Town

Edinburgh keeps many of its secrets well hidden. Pay a subterranean visit to the wynds and closes of the Old Town by joining Mercat Tours on one of its award-winning wanders through the deepest, most ancient vaults in the city.

 Scottish Poetry Library
Old Town

Just off the Canongate you'll spy the bookish confines of the Scottish Poetry Library, which holds fairly regular afternoon and evening events. The library itself is free to use, but you'll need to register online first at scottishpoetrylibrary.org.uk. Tours can also be arranged.

 Edinburgh Bus Tours
Old Town

This tried and tested company offers a variety of different sightseeing tours around the city on hop-on, hop-off buses. For first-time visitors, it's a valuable way of getting your bearings.

 Edinburgh Saints & Sinners Walking Tours
Old Town

Walking guide Peter Hamilton has extensive experience of leading visitors to the most fascinating parts of the city, sharing his local expertise while bringing the past to life. Private and group tours are both available.

 The Banshee Labyrinth Cinema
Old Town

Billed as Scotland's most haunted pub – prepare for grisly tales aplenty – the Banshee Labyrinth also holds weekly and monthly cinema events, with alternative and horror flicks being shown alongside more mainstream movies.

Harry Potter, Haggis & Horrible Histories
Old Town

This wonderfully alliterative tour takes in a crowd-pleasing selection of different Edinburgh quirks, incorporating everything from JK Rowling to Greyfriars Bobby. There's even the chance to tuck into a deep-fried Mars Bar at the end.

Activities

Victoria Street

Potter Trail

Now running for more than a decade, this highly rated Harry Potter-themed trail meanders around some of the most scenic parts of the city, taking in the café where JK Rowling penned the first Potter book, the real-life Diagon Alley, the resting place of He Who Must Not Be Named, and much more besides. Owls and broomsticks optional.

The Scotch Whisky Experience
Old Town

Get your tastebuds around the national firewater with a visit to this Royal Mile attraction, which has been lauding the joys of Scotch whisky for more than three decades. The tours are as lively and informative as you'd expect.

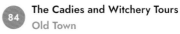

The Cadies and Witchery Tours
Old Town

Edinburgh has never been a stranger to ghostly goings-on, and on these Old Town walking tours you'll hear spooky tales of phantoms, fiends and the felons of the past. In addition to these early-evening walks, the same operator also runs tours of Greyfriars Cemetery – again with an emphasis on grisly tales.

The Ghost Bus Tours
Old Town

Billed as the UK's only comedy-horror theatre experience on wheels, this lively bus jaunt provides a city tour out of the norm. It takes in all the main sights, but puts an entertaining ghostly spin on the subject matter.

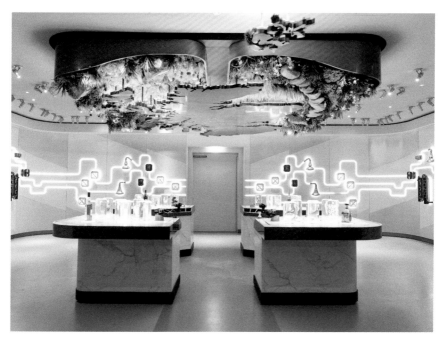

Johnnie Walker Experience - The Journey of Flavour Tour

Activities

 Johnnie Walker Princes Street
New Town

Time for a dram, highball, or a cocktail. This slick eight-floor venue offers a whole host of unmissable experiences, including immersive personalised tours, tastings, history adventures, retail and so much more. Catering for the curious right up to the connoisseur, expect an epic selection of drams, including many exclusives, with plenty for non-whisky fans and teetotallers to enjoy too.

Relax in one of two stunning rooftop bars, the 1820 Bar with unrivalled views of Edinburgh Castle and a seriously creative cocktail menu, or the Explorers' Bothy, home to STIR, the ground-breaking whisky and small bites pairing experience created in partnership with two Michelin-Starred Raby Hunt. A must visit, whether you're a whisky lover or not.

63

Leith Taproom Tour
Leith

Join this walking tour to get an overview of Leith's past and present through the worthy medium of beer. The tour takes in three brewery taprooms and includes a walk along the Water of Leith. Cheers to that.

 Port of Leith Distillery Tour
Leith

Billed as Scotland's first vertical distillery – it's set over nine floors of a remarkable building – this new Leith venture now offers 90-minute tours, giving the lowdown on its whisky-making process and letting you sample its new-make spirit.

DID YOU KNOW?

Alexander Graham Bell, the man credited with inventing the very first practical telephone, was born right here in Edinburgh, in 1847.

 Leith Farmers Market
Leith

Open from 10am to 5pm every Saturday, this local farmers market is where to head for your fill of bread, fresh meats and veg, home bakes, artisan goodies and more. There's plenty of street food on offer too, making it a good option for lunch.

 Trainspotting Tour
Leith

Irvine Welsh's cult book – and the subsequent film starring Ewan McGregor – were breakout cultural hits of the 1990s. Much of the action takes place in Leith, and occasional tours are offered of the locations immortalised on screen. The book *Choose Life, Choose Leith: Trainspotting on Location*, by Tim Bell, is a fascinating guide in its own right.

 Custom House
Leith

Scotland's oldest Custom House is still quite a sight, with its Georgian façade stretching over the harbourside. These days, however, it's a lively creative hub with resident artists and makers, as well as an exhibition space.

The Royal Yacht Britannia

92 **The Royal Yacht Britannia**
Leith

Britannia was Queen Elizabeth II's floating palace. The Yacht spent over 44 years in service, from 1954 to 1997, representing Britain, hosting state functions and acting as an ambassador for British business, promoting trade and industry around the globe with members of the Royal Family on board. The Britannia travelled over a million nautical miles in the process, calling at over 600 ports, but is now back in Scotland, the country where it was constructed.

Today it's one of the UK's best attractions, and a tour of the vessel takes in all five decks, from the State Apartments to the Crews' Quarters.

The Scotsman

Arts & Culture

Creativity runs through Edinburgh's veins, meaning arts and culture aplenty – this is, after all, a city that was named the top "cultural and creative city" of its size in Europe. The hard part for visitors is fitting it all in.

The Scottish Storytelling Centre

St Cecilia's Hall and Music Museum
Old Town

Sitting south of the Royal Mile, this is Scotland's oldest purpose-built concert hall. It's also home to Edinburgh university's remarkably impressive collection of musical instruments, showcasing everything from bagpipes and basset horns to harpsichords and hurdy-gurdies. The historical concert room hosts regular events.

 The Scottish Storytelling Centre
Old Town

An Old Town arts venue dedicated to the great Scottish art of spinning a tale, with workshops, exhibitions and storytelling as well as dance, music and theatre. Its modern frontage stands shoulder-to-shoulder with the John Knox House, a medieval dwelling with a layered history.

TIP

For a taste of tradition, visit the Haggis Box café inside the Scottish Storytelling Centre, celebrated for its classic Burns Supper experience.

 Festival Theatre
Old Town

David Bowie, Laurel and Hardy, Fats Domino and Charlie Chaplin are among those to have trodden the boards at this longstanding venue (known as the Festival Theatre only since 1994, but dating back as far as 1928). There's a seating capacity of more than 1,900, and the stage itself is Scotland's largest performance area.

 Andy Goldsworthy's Hutton Roof
Old Town

The roof of the National Museum of Scotland provides a lofty setting for this work by sculptor Andy Goldsworthy. Comprising a quartet of carved sandstone blocks, quarried from Dumfriesshire and representing the four points of the compass, the sculpture is partly inspired by the work of pioneering Edinburgh geologist James Hutton.

 Stills
Old Town

This photography-centred venue in the Old Town runs courses and events, as well as staging three major exhibitions a year.

Arts & Culture

Fruitmarket Gallery

Royal Lyceum Theatre
Old Town

Fruitmarket Gallery
Old Town

This is the city's leading dramatic playhouse, home to the widely respected Royal Lyceum Theatre Company and still staging a diverse range of plays, festival events and family productions, as well as various courses and workshops.

Always bang on trend, Fruitmarket is a well-reputed cultural venue in the heart of town, with exhibitions and events focused on contemporary art and culture. There's a bookshop and café alongside the exhibition spaces.

Scan here for more information on each listing. Enter the listing number to see our digital map, images and additional inspiration.

100 Scotsman Picturehouse
Old Town

Beneath the baroque bulk of the Scotsman Hotel – a fixture on North Bridge for more than a century – you'll find a cinema with a difference. 48 leather armchairs, complete with individual tables and empire lamps, gaze up towards a screen that shows a mixture of old classics and cult masterpieces. Trailers are kept to a minimum, so be sure to give yourself enough time to settle in with a cocktail.

101 Physicians' Gallery
New Town

Scotland's medical history comes under the stethoscope at this fascinating college exhibition space, which showcases rare books, vintage scientific illustrations, wax models and medicines. The gallery's open from Monday to Friday and needs no booking, but if you want to see the reading room and/or physic garden, prearrange a visit by emailing library@rcpe.ac.uk.

102 Embassy Gallery
New Town

Away from the big-name galleries and museums, Edinburgh has some bona fide artistic gems. On the edge of the New Town, this artist-run organisation, which puts on performances and exhibitions in its own space and elsewhere, is one of them.

103 Edinburgh Playhouse
New Town

The one and only. The Playhouse is the largest working theatre in the UK, its three levels holding more than 3,000 seats. Expect big-name musicals and big-budget plays. The venue is Grade I listed and was inspired by New York's Roxy Cinema.

104 Scottish National Gallery
New Town

Sitting on the Mound, close to Princes Street, the National boasts a high-class and extensive collection of priceless art, with works by the likes of Rembrandt, Titian, Constable and many more. Scottish painters such as Phoebe Anna Traquair and Henry Raeburn also figure heavily. Definitely not a place to be rushed through.

The Water of Leith

6 Times

The Water of Leith plays host to a permanent art installation – or, to be precise, half a dozen of them – with six of Antony Gormley's signature human sculptures dotted along its length. One of the works is actually found outside the Scottish National Gallery of Modern Art, with the other five standing in the water itself.

105 City Art Centre
New Town

Set in the heart of the city, just steps from Waverley Station, this nine-storey former warehouse showcases historic and contemporary Scottish visual and applied arts. Painting, photography and arts and crafts all get a look-in, and there's a regular programme of exhibitions.

106 The Scottish National Portrait Gallery
New Town

With a collection that encompasses everyone from Bonnie Prince Charlie to Emeli Sandé – and all housed in a vast neo-gothic bastion of red sandstone – this was the first purpose-built portrait gallery in the world when it opened in 1889. It's still a wonderful attraction.

107 Collective Gallery
New Town

Edinburgh locations don't come much more plum than an observatory on top of Calton Hill, but there's more to this unique contemporary art space than its setting. As well as running exhibitions and workshops, it also puts on artist-led activities for young people.

The Scottish National Portrait Gallery

 The Scottish National Gallery of Modern Art
Stockbridge

Made up of two separate venues – Modern One and Modern Two, which sit across the road from each other – these excellent galleries have a hugely impressive permanent collection, with sculpture-dotted grounds and large numbers of Dada and Surrealist works.

 Saorsa Gallery
Stockbridge

Saorsa (meaning Freedom in Gaelic) Gallery in Stockbridge might be small, but it packs a real punch. Inside you can find bold, vibrant works by owner and landscape artist Tommy Fitchet.

Scan here for more information on each listing. Enter the listing number to see our digital map, images and additional inspiration.

BirdsNest Gallery Meadows
Southside

The sister gallery to BirdsNest's main hub in Southside, this beautifully kooky exhibition space is set in an old police box on the east side of the Meadows. It calls itself Scotland's Smallest Gallery.

 Dovecot Studios
Southside

In situ for more than a century, this large-scale tapestry studio still makes superb rugs and tapestries and now doubles as a gallery and design museum, with regular events and exhibitions. There's a good café on site.

 Summerhall
Southside

Hosting everything from Fringe shows to Science Festival events, this arts complex and live venue also stages live music, theatre, cinema and more. It's based in a grand ex-university building near The Meadows, and has garnered a reputation as a ground-breaking arts hub.

 King's Theatre
West End

An ornate institution in place for well over a century, the King's has a lively programme of events year-round. West End-style shows are the norm.

 Edinburgh Printmakers
West End

Still, as its name suggests, a centre for printmaking, this inspiring venue has two galleries and a shop selling prints, as well as a studio space offering courses to all-comers.

 Traverse Theatre
West End

Staging diverse productions from visiting companies as well as present-day playwrights, this is where to come for serious drama and high-quality writing. It's always busy in the summer festival season.

Emma

TBCo

Leith

See page 144 for more information on TBCo.

Where is your favourite spot to enjoy a picnic in Edinburgh?

We live right by Portobello Beach so you will usually find me there with the kids running in and out of the sea covered in sand.

What local cafe would you be visiting to pick up your picnic goodies?

You can't beat fish and chips by the sea, and Shrimp Wreck at Portobello do a very good shrimp bun!

Can you recommend some must-see spots in your neighbourhood?

We spend a lot of time in Leith at our studio and love wandering down to the shore and having lunch at The Rose Leaf or dinner at our favourite restaurant Borough. You can also walk along the water of Leith which is beautiful and brings you out to Stockbridge where you can stop for some wine and cheese at Smith & Gertrude and the best ice cream at Jolato!

MUST SEE IN YOUR NEIGHBOURHOOD?

Leith Shore

The Rose Leaf

Borough

Water of Leith

Smith & Gertrude

Edinburgh's Most Famous Serial Killers

Scan here to listen to the audio reading

Back in the early 1800s, Edinburgh was at the forefront of modern medicine. However, it took a lot of fresh bodies to keep the anatomy classes running. When a change in the law resulted in a shortage of legal cadavers, some enterprising people saw an opportunity.

The theft of freshly buried corpses became so bad, that mourners were forced to protect their loved ones even after the funeral. Guardhouses and night watchmen were installed into graveyards as well as strong, iron mortsafes over fresh burials.

Burke and Hare, two of Edinburgh's most notorious residents, found a different way of doing business. William Hare ran a lodging house in Tanner's Close and, when one of his tenants died before he could pay the bill, he was determined to get his money somehow. Word had spread about the shortage of bodies for medical students and Hare had an idea.

With William Burke's help, he replaced the lodger's body in the coffin before it could be buried and carted it along to Surgeon's Square, selling it to anatomist Robert Knox. The assistant who handed over the cash made it very clear that if any other bodies turned up, they would be very welcome.

The pair could do with the extra income but getting hold of naturally occurring corpses wasn't an easy task. Instead, over the next 10 months, Burke and Hare murdered 16 people as part of their new enterprise.

Their usual technique was to lure the target back to Hare's lodging house, fill them with cheap whisky and suffocate them in a manner that would later be named "burking". While the bodies were still warm, they rushed them down the Cowgate to Knox's door.

Eventually, the pair were caught and Hare gave Burke up to save his own skin. In return for his full, written confession, Hare was released while his partner in crime was hanged and his body used for public dissection as poetic justice. Hare might have been a free man, but he was chased out of Edinburgh.

Nobody knows where he ended up or if he carried on his murderous enterprise somewhere new.

Stories

From Michelin-starred restaurants
to lip-smacking street vendors – via kooky
cafés, wood-panelled pubs and late-night
comfort food – Edinburgh keeps its visitors
well-fed and watered.

Food & Drink

Fhior

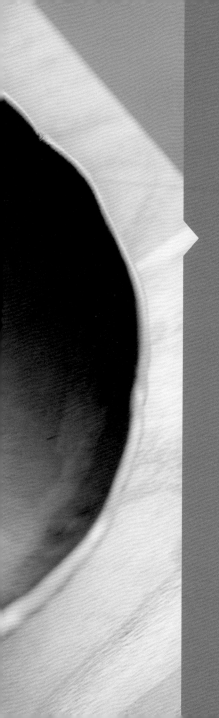

Restaurants

Eating out is one of the great joys
of an Edinburgh trip, whether
you're in search of high-quality
Scottish dining or tastebud-
blasting international dishes.
Pull up a chair and tuck in.

Wedgwood The Restaurant

 Timberyard
Old Town

 **Wedgwood The Restaurant**
Old Town

Behind a huge red door in the shadow of the castle, this historic 19th-century costume and prop warehouse and former timber yard now houses one of the capital's most exciting and inventive restaurants. Impressed by dishes such as "wild garlic broth and auld reekie steamed bun' and 'parfait, cylindra beetroot, cherry blossom & sweet cicely", the Radford family also bagged a Michelin star in 2023.

This Royal Mile restaurant established in 2007 takes the ubiquitous local, seasonal ingredients ethos one step further by taking diners on a journey to the source. Chef Paul Wedgwood offers two-hour foraging experiences in East Lothian followed by a tasting lunch back at the restaurant. More conventional dining experiences are also offered, the a la carte and tasting menus changing four times a year with the seasons.

**White Horse Oyster
& Seafood Bar**
Old Town

Pull up a stool at the bar for oyster happy hour, weekdays from 4-5pm and all afternoon on Sunday. In a revamped 18th-century inn at the bottom of the Royal Mile, this cosy little joint with its exposed stone walls and plush velvet banquettes also dishes up small plates, such as a crab Scotch egg with wasabi mayo and monkfish satay along with seafood sharing platters.

Soul Vegan
Old Town

A cracking vegan Malaysian restaurant in the city centre, where specialties include mapo tofu, pineapple fried rice and mushrooms in a ginger and wine broth. The chefs know their stuff.

Chop House
Old Town, Southside & Leith

A hip Scottish bar and butchery, there are three outposts of this mini restaurant chain, the first in Leith in a former cork warehouse, the second under the old railway arches near Waverley Station, the third in bonnie Bruntsfield. The design has an industrial vibe, the menu showcasing the best of British beef, butchered and dry-aged in house.

Ondine Oyster & Grill
Old Town

An Old Town institution, the award-winning Ondine Oyster & Grill was launched by chef Roy Brett in 2009 and has been showcasing the best sustainable Scottish seafood and shellfish ever since – with a global twist. The fish soup features flavours from North Africa and the local Dunbar crab risotto is laced with Spanish saffron.

Restaurants

Scan here for more information on each listing. Enter the listing number to see our digital map, images and additional inspiration.

Aizle

The Witchery

 The Witchery
Old Town

For dinner with a dramatic backdrop you can't beat James Thomson's legendary restaurant at the top of the Royal Mile. In the shadow of the castle, the 16th-century dining room is all plush ox blood-red leather banquettes, ornate wood-panelling, tapestries and candlelight while the Secret Garden dining room has a hand-painted ceiling. On the menu are old-school classics such as lobster thermidor, sole meuniere and their signature beef tartare.

 Makars Mushroom Emporium - Makars Mash Bar
Old Town

An underground mushroom emporium in the heart of the city? Well, why not? The basement of Makars Gourmet Mash Bar has been turned into a UV-lit fungi den, the produce of which ends up being used in some of its dishes. Diners can pop down before or after their meal to see the lair, which is decorated with psychedelic artwork.

85

Edinburgh Street Food

BABA

Aizle
New Town

In the leafy garden courtyard of the Kimpton Hotel on Charlotte Square, Stuart Ralston takes diners on a gastronomic adventure. The original premise set aside the traditional menu for a list of seasonal ingredients with no hint about their transcendental journey from field to tasting menu fork. The eight-course menu celebrates each season's "harvest", which in spring means slender spears of young asparagus, wild garlic, langoustines, lovage and lamb.

L'Escargot Bleu
New Town

Good neighbourhood French food from snails in garlic butter to braised beef cheeks in red wine and mussels and monkfish mariniere. A pocket of France on buzzing Broughton Street, this classic bistro was founded by legendary French chef Fred Berkmiller in 2009.

Scan here for more information on each listing. Enter the listing number to see our digital map, images and additional inspiration.

Fhior
New Town

The Gaelic word for 'true', Fhior's philosophy is spelt out in its name. Scot and Laura Smith's restaurant opened in 2018 vowing to stay true to their producers, the fishermen, farmers and foragers and the integrity of the fiercely seasonal ingredients, the sublime tasting menu served up in simple stream-lined surroundings has true culinary wow factor.

Edinburgh Street Food
New Town

Fact: Edinburgh does good street food. Sit-down restaurants are all good and well, but when hunger calls, sometimes all that's needed is an independent stall that does a few flavour-packed specialties.

BABA
New Town

Middle Eastern mezze and feasting dishes designed for sharing: this buzzing restaurant in the Kimpton Hotel on Charlotte Square dishes up platters of moreish mezze from BABA ganoush with pomegranate and mint to hot smoked trout, burnt lemon yoghurt and charred guindillas along with venison and urfa pepper carpaccio, whipped feta, pistachio dukkah and pickled shallots.

Noto

Café Royal

 Noto
129 New Town

 Café Royal
130 New Town

Stuart Ralston took a more relaxed approach for his second restaurant in 2019, substituting the tasting menu concept for small sharing plates and casual all-day dining. Noto, inspired by his time in New York – and named after Ralston's old roommate – dishes up Asian-tinged dishes such as ox cheek bao buns with onion and star anise and gnocchi, wild garlic, miso, shitakes and watercress.

This ornately tiled Victorian pub and seafood restaurant is famous for its oysters, served cold with either a mignonette or chilli, lime, and gin sauce; alternatively, served hot, panko-fried with purple dulse seaweed and citrus mayonnaise, or with Guinness, breadcrumbs, and crabmeat. Also on the menu is a medley of Scottish seafood staples from Cullen skink to seared scallops, classic fish pie, grilled lobster with roast garlic butter and rosemary fries, with crab bisque linguine.

131 New Town Fox
New Town

A strong option for a meal out in the New Town, with breakfast, lunch and dinner all on offer and plenty of veggie options. Expect the likes of smoked haddock pakora and glazed tempura cauliflower alongside burgers, full breakfasts and more.

132 The Lookout by Gardener's Cottage
New Town

Far removed from the Gardener's Cottage's rustic style, Dale Mailley's sleek, glass cantilevered box on top of Calton Hill dishes up panoramic views of the city's skyline and exquisite set three-course lunch and five-course evening menus, with or without matched drinks - plant-based and pescetarian available.

The Lookout by Gardener's Cottage

133 Café St Honoré
New Town

Down a cobbled alley parallel to Princes Street, this little restaurant is a quintessential French bistro, its name a nod to the patron saint of bakers and pastry chefs, the cooking style firmly French. It's been a favourite here since 2008, with chef Neil Forbes' daily changing menu showcasing the best of Scotland's seasonal and sustainable produce.

134 The Gardener's Cottage
New Town

A rustic country cottage in the heart of the city, with communal tables, a set menu and earthy ingredients – many grown steps from the door in the vegetable and herb patch. This was once the Royal Terrace's gardener's pretty stone cottage. The provenance of the produce is name-checked on the menu from Dunbar crab and herb tart to Isle of Gigha halibut and mussels with parsnip, apple, dill and truffle.

Restaurants

Tipo

 136 **Lucky Yu**
New Town

The pink neon sign is like a beacon on Broughton Street guiding diners to one of the hottest tables in town. Chef Duncan Adamson takes Asian-inspired street food to a new level, dishing up specialty dumplings, homemade baos and yakitori alongside a range of curated cocktails and natural wines. Inside the design inspiration is "wabi-sabi meets neon Tokyo" according to co-owner and designer Meredith Wilkie. Imagine "ancient Japanese artistry and urban neon glamour had a love child".

 137 **Tipo**
New Town

Restaurant number three in Stuart Ralston's stable, Tipo opened in spring 2023 on the first floor of a New Town townhouse, this time focusing on flavours from the Mediterranean, with homemade pastas and aged and cured charcuterie and cheeses. Think octopus carpaccio, duck liver parfait with walnut and fig and pappardelle with crab and chilli.

 135 **Hendersons**
New Town

Hendersons on Hanover Street was an Edinburgh institution, the city's original vegetarian restaurant dating back to 1962 and a New Town fixture until it closed in 2020. Now Barrie, the grandson of founder Janet Henderson, is carrying on the family tradition with a vegetarian and vegan restaurant updated for the 21st century in Tollcross. The interiors are light and contemporary, the lentil lasagne reimagined.

Hendersons

Something for all the family

recommended by @mylittleedinburgh

Makars Mash Bar
Old Town

Mums Comfort Food
Old Town

The Story Telling Centre
Old Town

Down The Hatch
New Town

City Restaurant
Southside

138 **Novapizza Vegan Kitchen**
Stockbridge

Run by a family from Rome, this small restaurant produces vegan versions of classic Italian pizzas and pastas. Lasagna, calzone, bolognese – it's all here. Need more convincing? It was named Vegan Restaurant of the Year in 2021 at the Food Awards Scotland.

139 **Eòrna**
Stockbridge

Chef Brian Grigor and sommelier Glen Montgommery launched their sophisticated two-man show in 2023, a 12-seater countertop chef's table with an ever-evolving seasonal tasting menu paired with classic old-world wines. Think Mull cheddar mousse with quince and hazelnut alongside Belhaven smoked salmon, lemon purée, quails egg and caviar.

Scan here for more information on each listing. Enter the listing number to see our digital map, images and additional inspiration.

Earls Burger Co.

 **Earls Burger Co.**
Stockbridge

 Skua
Stockbridge

A sticky icky or a dirty south? The first is a 4oz smashed pattie with sticky braised brisket, beer-battered onion rings, American cheese doused in Gorgonzola ranch, the second, two smashed patties, crispy smoked bacon, waffle fries and BBQ sauce with guidilla pepper. This hip fast food joint in Stockbridge gives the burger a gourmet twist.

The second restaurant from chefs Tomás Gormley and Sam Yorke, whose Leith-based restaurant Heron bagged a Michelin star in 2023, Skua, in a Stockbridge basement, is more of a dimly lit late-night dining spot dishing up seasonally inspired curated small plates. Think trout pastrami with furikake, taramasalata and rye along with fried chicken with fermented peach and pork belly sando, sweet chilli and kimchi.

Harajuku Kitchen
Southside

Expect AA rosette-level Japanese cuisine at this brilliant family restaurant, which specialises in authentic sushi and gyoza dumplings. The weekday lunch offers are particularly good value. The main restaurant is on Gillespie Place, with a smaller street food option in St James Quarter.

Junk
Southside

Now here's somewhere that understands the power of tasty grub. The family behind Junk have fine dining backgrounds and made their name through prize-winning street food – their Newington-based bar and restaurant, complete with cocktails, is the real deal.

Rhubarb
Southside

A decadent, fine-dining den in an opulent, historic hotel on the leafy edge of Edinburgh. Prestonfield was the first estate in Scotland to propagate rhubarb and it's still grown in the kitchen garden - and a star of the pudding menu: Rhubarb Gateau St Honore with white chocolate sherbet. This is the kind of place to splash out on the chateaubriand and a good claret.

Kanpai
West End

If you're hankering after a soft shell crab roll, slithers of glistening Scottish salmon, sea bass or shrimp sashimi or hot-off-the-griddle grilled aubergine in a sweet miso sauce, head to this sleekly designed Japanese restaurant in the city's West End.

No.35 at The Bonham
West End

Part of The Bonham Hotel, this wood-panelled restaurant not only serves up top-tier seasonal produce but offers some seriously swish design touches. One for a special night out. The hotel does impressive afternoon teas too, with the option to add champagne.

Dulse
West End

Sip a Dulse martini, a seaweed-salty cocktail with a spoonful of caviar on the side in the ground floor bar, then head upstairs to tuck into small sharing plates such as the signature lobster crumpet or Arbroath Smokie Tart - with dulse seaweed - in chef Dean Banks' relaxed seafood-focused neighbourhood restaurant in Edinburgh's West End.

Kanpai

Forage and Chatter

Rhubarb

Forage and Chatter
West End

The clue's in the name. Many of the ingredients on the menu in this low-key little basement restaurant are foraged, the vibe relaxed. Tuck into dishes such as Orkney scallop ceviche, cucumber, crème fraiche, fennel and roe followed by pearl barley risotto with garlic, walnut pesto and corra linn.

Kyloe
West End

At Kyloe, savour the finest in Scottish beef cuisine. Head Chef John Rutter and his team carefully select and prepare traditional and unique cuts of beef. From the drama of tableside carving to award-winning Sunday Roasts, Kyloe offers a memorable dining experience.

Pizzeria 1926
West End

Pegged as the authentic taste of Naples, this laidback little pizza joint dishes up traditional starters such as "arancini", the rice balls dusted with breadcrumbs and served with a spicy tomato dip as well as puffy-crusted, wood-fired pizzas loaded with fresh ingredients such as the zielinksi, topped with tomato, provola, basil, parmesan and fried aubergine.

Yamato
West End

Sister outlet to Kanpai, Yamato is an equally polished Japanese restaurant on a Tollcross side-street. The striking exterior, granite grey panels and natural wood is mirrored by the interiors' uncluttered lines, with intricate cut-out partitions between tables, delicate pink and white light shades resembling modernist flowers for a natural motif.

Restaurants

Scan here for more information on each listing. Enter the listing number to see our digital map, images and additional inspiration.

Vegan friendly eateries

recommended by @sarahscotland

Paradise Palms
Dalry

The Sly Fox
Leith

Nova Pizza
Old Town

Soul Vegan
Southside

The Bonham
West End

 152 **Heron**
Leith

Overlooking the Water of Leith, this much-lauded newcomer was awarded a Michelin star this year. The two talented young chef-owners, Tomás Gormley and Sam Yorke, dish up farm-to-table fine dining with an a la carte and tasting menu in pared-back contemporary surroundings.

 153 **The Little Chartroom**
Leith

Roberta Hall-McCarron and husband Stuart McCarron outgrew their bijoux base on Leith Walk, moving to roomier premises in what was once Michelin-starred chef Martin Wishart's cook school. Rave reviews have continued to flood in for starters such as beef tartare, smoked beef fat, quails egg, caper jam, cured ox heart and mains such as cod, asparagus, brown shrimp and potato nori.

 154 **Knights Kitchen**
Leith

Chrisine Knights' home-cooked, largely plant-based Kenyan soul food is a popular Edinburgh pit stop. Queues snake out the door for the fragrant lentil dahl, chickpea and spinach coconut curry, mandazi and North African date scones.

Knights Kitchen

 Restaurant Martin Wishart
Leith

For old-school, white table-clothed elegance head to The Shore in Leith and Edinburgh-born Martin Wishart's Michelin-starred eponymous restaurant. This is modern European fine dining with a selection of a la carte and tasting menus. Think dishes such as Scrabster turbot with white asparagus, morels, salt-baked celeriac and truffle cream alongside roast saddle of Dornoch lamb, crispy belly, Wye valley asparagus, pomme salardaise, tomato and thyme jus.

 The Kitchin
Leith

Tom Kitchin's Michelin-starred restaurant down in Leith's revamped docklands has been a stalwart on Edinburgh's dining scene since it opened in 2006, the philosophy "From Nature to Plate" leading the way, the signature "Pig's Head and Langoustine" now legendary. He also has a gastropub, the Scran and Scallie in villagey Stockbridge, neighbourhood restaurant Kora in Bruntsfield and, outside Edinburgh, in the seaside village of Gullane, The Bonnie Badger, a restaurant with rooms.

157 Razzo Pizza
Leith

Cool and contemporary - think brick tiles and stool seating - this narrow Neapolitan pizzeria is a popular Leith eatery. As well as classic flavour combos such as the Margherita and Marinara, check out the seasonal specials such as Fiori di Zucca Acciughe e Burrata - zucchini flowers, rich, creamy Pugliese burrata and salty anchovies, drizzled with extra virgin olive oil - or Salsiccia e Friarielli, a white pizza with smoked provola cheese, Sicilian sausage and friarielli (leafy greens). To finish? Sicilian cannolo, a crisp sweet tube of pastry, oozing ricotta cream and dusted with pistachios.

Razzo Pizza

 158 Nobles Café Bar & Restaurant
Leith

This family-owned, revamped Victorian bar dishes up great gastropub grub. Alongside the usual suspects such as beer-battered Peterhead haddock and chips and steak frites there's miso-marinated roast aubergine with kimchi fried rice. The fries are loaded with truffle and parmesan or rosemary salted, the ice-cream homemade.

 159 Borough
Leith

Chef Darren Murray took over this corner spot in Leith in 2019 and survived the lengthy lockdowns by making Michelin-lauded gourmet pies. Now back on track, the restaurant, with its pared-back, pale wood interiors, offers an a la carte menu featuring dishes such as fried aubergine, olive, dill, preserved lemon and the odd pie: chicken Leith sherry and mushroom with barbecued leeks,

Safraz & Jemma

Beatnik

West End

See page 128 for more information on Beatnik.

MUST SEE IN YOUR NEIGHBOURHOOD?

The Wildcat

Hey Palu

Alby's

Argyle Place

Where's your favourite place to grab a bite to eat in the neighbourhood?

Argyle Place is our go to. The space is so beautifully thought out. Bright, airy. The staff are amazing, they often come into BEATNIK. The food menu is really well thought out, they have an insane pastry section which often changes too.

Where is the best spot to enjoy one of your coffees?

On our bench outside! It's such a good people watching spot. It's shielded by the neighbouring hedge, as well as our awning towering over you above, so you're perfectly protected from the elements. You can hear the music bop and the buzz from BEATNIK, but also the hustle from the street.

The Canny Man's

Bars

Edinburgh has more pubs and
bars per capita than almost
anywhere else in the world (only
Las Vegas, Prague and Orlando
have more) – so the only sensible
thing to do is to raise a glass.

The World's End

The World's End
Old Town

Dragonfly
Old Town

The name isn't the cheeriest, but it's not a prediction of the apocalypse, more a nod to the fortress mentality that existed here after the Scottish defeat at the Battle of Flodden in 1513. The exterior of this traditional 16th-century pub at the foot of the Royal Mile nudged up to the Flodden Wall, which once circled and protected Edinburgh's Old Town. Outside the walls it was another world.

Edinburgh's cocktail revival, they say, started here. On an Old Town back street, the décor's eclectic, the playlists genre-spanning and the cocktails ever-evolving. A herbaceous and complex 'Plum & Dandy' marries spirits from one of the oldest centres of Scottish distilling, Lindores Abbey, with one of the newest, Copenhagen's Empirical, seasoned with chamomile and hops and topped with plum 'leather'.

The Banshee Labyrinth
Old Town

Proudly known as the most haunted pub in Scotland, this club is partly located in vaults once traipsed by criminals and unsavouries – and the other is located in the home of one of Edinburgh's richest former residents. Enjoy karaoke or one of many live gigs in the bar or head further in to discover their on-site cinema.

Salt Horse
Old Town

A contemporary craft beer shop and bar rather than an old-timers' pub, there are 14 keg lines and 250 bottled beers on the menu, a rustic beer garden where you can "drink outside in the wind and rain", and if you get the munchies they do a good lineup of burgers and chips.

The Devil's Advocate
Old Town

If you find yourself on Advocate's Close, just off Edinburgh's Royal Mile, you might be tempted to pop into this trendy cocktail bar. Located in a disused Victorian pump station, it has rustic yet modern interiors. A large selection of whiskies are on offer, as well as some devilishly tasty whisky cocktails.

The Banshee Labyrinth

Bars

Holyrood Distillery Courtyard
Old Town

Edinburgh's first city centre whisky distillery to open in over a century, Holyrood Distillery was founded in 2019 in an old railway terminus and listed building. Along with distillery tours and tastings there's a contemporary bar with a killer view of Arthur's Seat, where you can sip a bespoke cocktail or take a gin or whisky flight.

Jolly Judge

SCOTCH Whisky Bar
Old Town

Set in the luxurious Balmoral Hotel and home to a hand-crafted oak cabinet containing more than 500 single malts, you'll find all the main Scottish whisky regions well represented – and in stylish surrounds, too.

Jolly Judge
Old Town

This independent old-school boozer, with its low-beamed ceilings and a roaring fire in the shadow of the castle, is as cosy as it sounds. There's a rotating list of craft beers and ciders as well as real ales on tap.

Deacon Brodie's Tavern

Deacon Brodie's Tavern
Old Town

A Royal Mile fixture, this legendary 19th-century pub with its ornately carved ceiling is named after Deacon William Brodie, born in 1741 and said to be one of the characters that inspired Robert Louis Stevenson's novel *The Strange Case of Dr Jekyll and Mr Hyde*. By day, Brodie was a respected carpenter, by night he turned to crime and burglary to pay off his drinking and gambling debts.

Bellfield Brewery
Near Old Town

Sometimes a quality gluten-free beer can be hard to pin down but at Bellfield Brewery, all its beer is gluten-free. Brewing an extensive range of delicious ales, IPAs, pilsners and lagers, customers are never short on choice and can even taste seasonal specials from other breweries. Its team says it's all about "exceptional beer, no exceptions".

Bramble
New Town

Late-night drinking den and cult speakeasy basement bar, Bramble is a subterranean hideaway, all low lighting, cosy armchairs and innovative cocktails. It was the first venue launched by Edinburgh entrepreneurs Mike Aikman and Jason Scott, who now have two others in their stable - as well as their own drinks company, Mothership.

The Black Cat
New Town

This rustic, independent bar on cobbled Rose Street has one of the largest whisky collections in the city, an eclectic mismatched tables and banquettes vibe and great live folk music.

Lucky Liquor Co.
New Town

The third bar from Mike Aikman and Jason Scott took its design inspiration from Europe's café-bar culture with its striking black and white tiled floor and retro Bentwood chairs. Its USP is the seasonally evolving menu of 13 cocktails, based on the 13 base spirits behind the bar. It changes every three months – or 13 weeks.

Lady Libertine
New Town

One for cocktail connoisseurs, this glamorous haunt is in the basement - and the ground floor - of the Edinburgh Grand on St Andrew Square. The upstairs section has high ceilings and a long art deco-inspired bar. Downstairs in the old bank vaults (this was once the Royal Bank of Scotland's headquarters) it's dark and decadent, all columns, retro tasselled lamps, and a dramatic backlit bar where the mixologists whip up creative concoctions.

Pickles
New Town

On buzzing Broughton Street, this rustic little wine bar has shelves lined with preserves and pickles and dishes up platters of pungent pâtés (from venison to wild boar), Mediterranean meats and Scottish cheeses to go with the carefully curated wine list and bottled beers.

Scan here for more information on each listing. Enter the listing number to see our digital map, images and additional inspiration.

Lucky Liquor Co.

Lady Libertine

Spry

Pickles

The Oxford Bar
New Town

One for fans of Ian Rankin's Rebus novels, the Oxford Bar is a favourite haunt of the fictional detective - and his creator. Down a cobbled alley close to Charlotte Square, it's a traditional old-world, bare-bones boozer - nothing fancy, the place to sup a pint in front of the fire and chat to the locals.

The Bon Vivant
New Town

The Bon Vivant in Edinburgh's New Town is a stylish bar celebrated for its extensive cocktail and wine offerings. Known for its relaxed yet indulgent atmosphere, it's a favourite for its expertly mixed drinks, including whisky cocktails, and its vast selection of wines served in a setting of soft lighting and intimate booths.

Panda & Sons
New Town

Panda & Sons, disguised as a vintage barbershop, is a speakeasy-style cocktail haven in Edinburgh. Since its 2013 launch, it's famed for its theatrical setting and ingenious cocktails, presented in a storybook-style menu spanning six chapters of mixology artistry.

Kay's Bar
New Town

A bijou bolthole and Edinburgh institution on the corner of a cobbled street in the Georgian New Town, this tiny Victorian pub, once a wine merchant, has a beer-barrel-meets-red-velvet-boudoir vibe and cosy backroom where you can play a game of Scrabble.

Spry
New Town

This pared-back neighbourhood wine bar and bottle shop specialises in natural wines and serves a la carte and five-course set menus. Think Jerusalem artichokes with cavolo nero and pickled pear, steamed crab bun with buckwheat and coriander or rolled pork belly with apple and gremolata.

The Last Word Saloon
Stockbridge

Sister establishment to Bramble and the Lucky Liquor Co., the Last Word Saloon is a vintage-chic, sheepskin-strewn basement bar on St Stephen Street in Stockbridge, the eponymous "Last Word" cocktail a heady concoction of gin, green Chartreuse, maraschino liqueur and fresh lime juice.

Bars

Smith & Gertrude
181 Stockbridge

'Wine. Cheese. Company' is the ethos. When Amy and Duncan Findlater opened this hip hangout it was a departure for traditional Stockbridge. The interiors are eclectic: think reclaimed wooden school-gym floors, communal tables, an old record player in the corner and a stack of vinyl. The wide-angled wine list features natural, organic and biodynamic releases while the wine flights showcase left-field vintages from "the wrong side of the tracks". On the food menu you'll find local platters of cheese and charcuterie.

Smith & Gertrude

 The Canny Man's
182 Southside – Morningside

Once notorious for its curmudgeonly landlord - if he didn't like the look of you, he wouldn't serve you - now the Canny Man's is more universally welcoming. An Edinburgh institution since 1871, it's a family-run, independent old-school boozer, famous for its Bloody Marys and proclaimed "the best pub in the world" by Rick Stein.

 The Abbey
183 Southside

You'll find fine drams by the hundred at this traditional whisky bar near The Meadows, south of the city centre. And if whisky's not your thing? It also does great cask ale, not to mention a full food menu.

 Scan here for more information on each listing. Enter the listing number to see our digital map, images and additional inspiration.

The Wildcat
West End – Tollcross

Home to the legendary £5 Negroni, this cool cocktail bar has a ballsy attitude and off-the-wall drinks list. Take a punt on the House Gibson: Electric Spirit gin and Cuciela Bianco packed with pickled onions. It also serves classic cocktails, the odd dram and a glass or two of fine wine.

Hey Palu
West End – Tollcross

A hip Italian cocktail and wine bar on Bread Street where you can take a negroni flight: straight up, wild strawberry (Scottish gin, bitter bianco, wild strawberry, dry vermouth) and caffe cyroni (Cuban rum, amaro, bitter, coffee beans). Other signature classics include the yuzu margarita and the Godfather – a 'short and dangerous' mix of single malt whisky, amaretto and apricot.

The Rat Pack Piano Bar
West End

This Shandwick Place bar is a classy drinking hole where the mood's retro and the main attraction is music played live on a grand piano – expect hits from the past and the present.

Lost in Leith
West End

An atmospheric vaulted beer hall with barrel-aged brews from owners Campervan Brewery, as well as other quality beers and spirits from Scotland and worldwide. They don't do hot food, but pizzas can be delivered from Pizza Geeks across the road.

Teuchters Landing
Leith

This dockside pub in Leith is all about whisky, beer and location – it's set in what was once the waiting room for the Leith to Aberdeen steamboat ferry, and its beer garden and pontoon have great waterside views.

Nauticus
Leith

This classy Leith pub is one you'll want to linger in, with its dark wood panelling, nautical décor and – best of all – a Scottish-influenced cocktail list for the ages, ranging from the Leith Sherry Wobbler to the Porridge Colada.

Bars

A dram in the city

recommended by @singlemaltmark

The Athletic Arms
Dalry

Nauticus
Leith

Scotch at The Balmoral
Old Town

The Abbey Bar
Southside

The Ensign Ewart
Old Town

190 **Mistral**
Leith

Neighbourhood wine bar and bottle shop in one, this cool little spot dishes up small plates and carefully curated wines from independent producers. The menu includes cheese, charcuterie and paired wines, along with the usual suspects: bread, olives - and oysters.

191 **Satyr**
Leith

From the team behind the Wildcat Bar, Satyr on Leith Walk slings classic cocktails seven days a week, 4pm till late. Also on the menu are craft beers and wines from small-scale producers - mouth-watering meat and cheese boards on the side.

192 **Roseleaf Bar Café**
Leith

At this gastropub, the cocktails come in teapots - 'pot-tails' - and the bar showcases some of Leith's best brewers: Campervan's Leith Juice is an IPA packed with hops and orange zest while Pilot's Peach Melba Sour is a tart dessert-inspired beer.

Mistral

 193 Bittersweet
Leith

 194 The Port of Leith Distillery
Leith

Artisan distiller and mixologist Fabrizio Cioffi and his brother, Simone, a chef, launched this cool street corner cocktail bar-meets-modern Italian eaterie, to introduce Edinburgh to the art of aperitivo. Nearby Fabrizio's Leith-based craft distillery, Old Poison, produces rum, gin and botanical-based aperitifs and offers tours and tastings.

Sitting almost at the very top of Scotland's first vertical distillery, the Port of Leith Distillery Bar serves cocktails nearly as beautiful as the sweeping view over the city, best enjoyed alongside their carefully curated small plates menu.

 Scan here for more information on each listing. Enter the listing number to see our digital map, images and additional inspiration.

CREME
BRULEE

BLUEBERRY
JAM
LEMON
POSSET

RASPBERRY
CHEESECAKE

Cafés

You're never far from a caffeine fix in the Scottish capital. Edinburgh has more than its share of artisan roasters and third wave coffee outlets. You can even take a barista course.

The Milkman

 **Hideout Café**
Old Town

There's a retro vibe at this family-run coffee shop hidden away off the Royal Mile in the shadow of Edinburgh Castle, the music played on an old-school tape deck. On the menu, a Pink Floyd smoothie (cherries, mango, apple juice and rhubarb) or a "Prince" (forest berries, almond milk, mint and honey) along with the usual modern suspects from flat whites to iced chai lattes.

 Room & Rumours
Near Old Town

Coffee and doughnuts, you say? Look no further for your caffeine and sugar hit than this coffee shop and Donutterie on East Market Street near Waverley Station – and don't miss the homemade sourdough bread.

 The Milkman
Old Town

Founder Mark's great-grandfather drove the last horse-drawn milk float in Aberdeenshire and his silhouette is the logo of this rustic little coffee shop, which showcases a rotating range of sustainable roasteries including Girls who Grind Coffee and Obadiah Collective.

 Union Brew Lab
Old Town

With two types of espresso and two filters every day from Union Hand-Roasted Coffees along with a handful of guest roasteries, this artisan café focuses on single-origin coffees. You can also sign up for one of their barista courses from an espresso masterclass to latte art class.

 Gordon Street Coffee
Old Town

This small-batch roastery was founded in Glasgow then spread its wings to an Old Town location hunkered beside Waverley Station. Try the Edinburgh Roast, the beans from Africa and Central America with hazelnut, chocolate and stone fruit notes.

 The Elephant House
Old Town

Appropriately located on Edinburgh's answer to Diagon Alley, the Elephant House Café made famous by JK Rowling has opened a second shop on Victoria Street. With a distinct Harry Potter theme you can even buy Butterscotch Beer from the cupboard under the stairs!

Cafés

Something Sweet

Mary's Milk Bar
201 Old Town

Homemade gelato is the name of the game at this excellent Grassmarket outlet, where owner Mary makes the goods herself, and makes the most of her background as chocolatier to offer other sweet treats too. The hot chocolate's a godsend on a chilly day.

Moo Pie Gelato
202 Old Town

Small-batch gelato doesn't come much tastier than at this artisan ice cream shop just off the Royal Mile. The Moo Pie itself is a scoop of gelato sandwiched between two freshly baked cookies – to which the only correct response is yes, please.

Alandas
203 Old Town

Making all its gelato at its onsite micro-factory, this ice cream parlour is a mere scamper away from the Greyfriars Bobby statue. All its flavours can also be served as creamy milkshakes.

Cairngorm Coffee Roasters
204 New Town

Clever dripper, piccolo, long black, flat white or batch brew? One for coffee connoisseurs, the beans roasted in the Cairngorm Coffee Roasters, owner Robi Lambie opted for different designs for the two cafés to set them apart from mainstream chains. Frederick Street's basement café is rustic, mountain chic with coffee sacks on the ceiling. Melville Place is all light, bright, high-tabled, blonde wood.

Lowdown
205 New Town

At low-key Lowdown in a Georgian terrace basement on George Street you can take a coffee flight: an espresso, piccolo and pour over. The sleek, minimalist interiors feature a marble and oak counter, more kitchen than café, with a rotating mix of guest roasteries.

Scan here for more information on each listing. Enter the listing number to see our digital map, images and additional inspiration.

Lowdown

Cairngorm Coffee Roasters

Room & Rumours

Ante
New Town

The talented team behind bottle shop and wine bar Spry upstairs have branched out into coffee - with huge slices of homemade cake and savoury specials such as parsnip pâté on toast, chorizo and fried egg brioche and langoustine Danish with bisque mousse devoured in this subterranean hideout.

Leo's Beanery
New Town

Named after owner Joe's grandfather (who didn't apparently like coffee), this New Town basement café has been dishing up hearty homemade food since 2004. Tuck into Leo's Croque-mon-scone, a halved cheese scone topped with parma ham and melted cheddar, or a hearty bowl of porridge with cinnamon maple toasted nuts, seeds and fruit.

Urban Angel
New Town

Serving Edinburgh for 15 years, Urban Angel is the heart of serious food. Indulge in classics like eggs benedict and French toast, along with nourishing smoothie bowls. Ethical sourcing, gluten-free, vegetarian and vegan options available.

Wellington Coffee
New Town

This tiny subterranean coffee spot on the corner of George and Hanover Street was one of the pioneers of Edinburgh's vibrant coffee scene, set up by hotshot barista Jonathan Sharp. There's a smattering of tables outside and rustic wood panelling and stool seating within, the coffee from London-based roaster Square Mile as well as local guest roasters.

Mayvn
New Town

Found inside the Eden Locke Hotel on George Street, Mayvn is one of the capital's best kept secrets. It's bright, fresh and welcoming, operating both as a work-friendly coffee shop and late-night café with good coffee guaranteed.

Artisan Roast
New Town, Southside & Leith

As Edinburgh coffee shops go, Artisan Roast is an institution with locations scattered around the city and a horde of dedicated customers. They've been roasting their own beans since 2007 and you can be sure that whichever shop you visit, they take their coffee very seriously.

Wellington Coffee

Afternoon Tea

recommended by @gisforgeorgina

Palm Court - The Balmoral
New Town

Georgian Tea Room - The Dome
New Town

Colonnades - Signet Library
Old Town

Lighthouse Restaurant - Fingal
Leith

The Witchery
Old Town

212 The Pantry
Stockbridge

Since 2012 Chris and Charlotte Thompson have been dishing up one of Edinburgh's best brunches, tables spilling out onto the pavement at this popular Stockbridge pit stop. The eggs benedict is near-legendary but the gooseberry fool French toast and Belgian waffles are tempting too.

213 Fortitude Coffee
Stockbridge

In the bustling heart of Stockbridge, an inviting coffee house blends vintage charm with modern flavours. The spacious venue offers a plethora of espressos, complemented by an assortment of freshly baked treats. Their retail offering includes an array of fine coffees, brew gear and exquisite loose leaf tea.

214 The Pastry Section
Stockbridge

Savoury-seekers walk on by says the blurb. It's all about sweet treats in the Pastry Section in Stockbridge. Swing by for freshly baked brownies, lemon meringue tarts and moreish snickerdoodle cookies. There's now also a second outlet in Leith.

The Pastry Section

 Cowan & Sons
215 Stockbridge

Behind the pretty stained glass windows is a popular family-run neighbourhood art gallery and café in quaint Stockbridge with banana bread bowls, artisan hot chocolate from Edinburgh-based Edward and Irwyn, and locally roasted Obadiah coffee.

 Grow Urban
216 Stockbridge and West End

Fight your way through the foliage in these pot plant shops to the coffee counter and order a cappuccino and cake while you browse and potter around the in-house potting shed. Botanical boutique and café for the urban gardener.

 Scan here for more information on each listing. Enter the listing number to see our digital map, images and additional inspiration.

Salt Café

 **Lannan Bakery**
Stockbridge

When Darcie Maher opened her first bakery on Hamilton Place in summer 2023 the hype was so huge there were queues along the street and the pastries sold out by mid-morning. Get there early for cute cardamom buns, squidgy custard slices and maple and pecan croissants.

 Salt Café
Southside

Salt Café, an acronym that encapsulates its philosophy - Seasonal, Artisanal, Local and Thoughtful - is an all-day brunch haven nestled in Morningside. Here, everything from the cakes to the butchery is handled in-house, ensuring top quality and freshness.

 Scan here for more information on each listing. Enter the listing number to see our digital map, images and additional inspiration.

Considerit
Southside

A plant-based pit stop by The Meadows offering hand-crafted vegan chocolates, ice-cream, milkshakes and oat milk cappuccinos with gooey treats from salted caramel cupcakes to pistachio yum yums and gourmet doughnuts, flavours ranging from lemon shortcake to blackcurrant jammy dodger and chocolate Oreo.

Argyle Place
Southside

Not far from the Meadows, Argyle Place is crisp, clean and very cool. While the specialist coffee is worth the visit alone, it's the food that's the real star here. Fresh, local ingredients are turned into real masterpieces that almost look too good to eat! Almost...

101 Bakery
Southside

This pot-plant-peppered little bakery does a fine line in fancy cakes, teetering, fresh-flower-topped, pastel-hued creations, but also dishes up sugary sweet snacks-to-go - think gooey cinnamon buns, banana and white chocolate cookies and salted caramel brownies.

Machina Coffee Roasters
Southside

Cool, contemporary speciality coffee spot - what happens when a music industry exec jumps ship, jets off on a research trip around the world to check out the coffee scene from Tokyo to LA and then launches his own café-roastery.

Castello Café
Southside

This turquoise-toned little café and popular brunch spot on Bruntsfield Links is all exposed brick walls and scuffed wooden floors. Think garlic mushrooms on sourdough, spicy huevos rancheros and stacks of sticky banoffee pancakes with Chantilly cream.

Black Medicine Coffee Co
Southside

Sitting on the corner of South Bridge, near the University of Edinburgh, Black Medicine is a popular spot for students to fuel their typing with caffeine. After recently celebrating its 25th year this busy coffee shop is sure to be around for 25 more.

Cafés

Dog Friendly

recommended by @theedinburghspaniels

Machina
Southside

Salt Café
Southside

Books n' Cup
West End

Hideout Café
Old Town

Lady and the Bear
Southside

 225 **Beatnik**
West End

A hip hangout and specialist coffee spot, with a minimalist, utilitarian vibe, the interiors coffee-toned, the walls a creamy latte, the metal stools espresso-hued with guest coffees from indie roasteries such as Edinburgh-based Obadiah and April Coffee from Copenhagen.

 226 **Café MILK**
West End

The holy trinity of MILK venues can be found at the Edinburgh Sculpture Workshop, in the West End and Inverleith Park. Tuck into maple miso mushroom on toast, washed down with a rosemary honey latte or a pot of oolong at the Sculpture Workshop. Or bag some banana bread, a breakfast brioche and Americano to go from the coffee shack in Inverleith park.

 227 **Throat Punch Coffee Company**
West End

What started out as an online business moved in to its first grown-up premises in 2021. Founded by a couple of coffee addicts, their first "offensively strong" Indian Cherry Robusta is still on the menu, all burnt sugar, smoky wood and maple aromatics for those craving a full-bodied caffeine kick.

Twelve Triangles

228 **Twelve Triangles**
Various Locations

Sourdough and sandwiches – the doorstop variety. The first branch of this artisan café opened in 2015 just off Leith Walk. Now there are eight across the city and one down in the Borders. Twelve Triangles specialises in slow-fermented sourdough but you can also bag a black charcoal loaf along with gourmet doughnuts and pastries.

229 **Williams & Johnson Coffee Co**
Leith

In their flagship café in Custom Lane, a cool, contemporary exhibition space and design hub on Leith's waterfront, you can learn about the roasting process – they roast the beans here on Mondays and Tuesdays – or just relax with a flat white.

 Scan here for more information on each listing. Enter the listing number to see our digital map, images and additional inspiration.

Toast
230 Leith

Discover Toast, Leith's vibrant wine café at The Shore. Indulge in imaginative dishes like huevos rancheros and Mediterranean-inspired small plates. Satisfy your cravings with artisan cakes and pastries, including vegan and gluten-free options. Raise a glass to warm conversations and a carefully curated wine list. Cheers to the pure enjoyment of eating and drinking with friends.

 **Printworks Coffee**
231 Leith

Another great little indie café supporting small food and drink producers, the coffee - sip a macchiato or moreish mocha - from Monmouth Coffee Company. On the menu a mouthwatering selection of pastries and paninis.

 **Boxwood Tam Bakery**
232 Leith

Based on Queen Charlotte Street, this superb little bakery produces the classics as well as less standard fare – come along to try anything from bicolour croissants and pastrami and cheese viennoiseries to Mikado twists and pain suisses.

 Albys
233 Leith

Alby's speciality is Big Hot Sandwiches, the moreish flavour combos including Sichuan Oyster Mushroom (fried oyster mushroom, Sichuan pepper, doubanjiang mayo, pickled mooli, pickled chilli, sticky onions and rocket) and Porchetta and 'Nduja with fennel and chilli porchetta, 'Nduja mayo, fennel and caper salad and rocket. There's now a second branch in Southside.

 **Babyfaced Baker**
234 Leith

Brilliant name, brilliant bakery. This Leith spot started out as a recipe blog, before baker Rhiain made the wise move of taking it one step further – she now sells the likes of Biscoff Nutella brownies and toffee and salted pretzel cookies on Leith Walk.

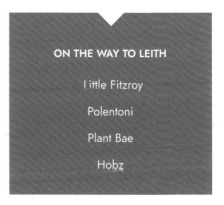

ON THE WAY TO LEITH

Little Fitzroy

Polentoni

Plant Bae

Hobz

Amanda
Potted Garden

Stockbridge

Keep an eye out for the charming potted garden as you wander along Circus Lane.

Edinburgh has a reputation for beautiful green spaces, could you recommend some that visitors absolutely shouldn't miss?

A must-visit is the Royal Botanic Garden Edinburgh, affectionately known as 'The Botanics'. It offers a blend of horticulture, history, and a great shop. For those seeking lesser-known spots, Scotland's Garden Scheme is a treasure trove. Gardens across the city, including the Open Gardens of Stockbridge and Lower New Town, open their gates to the public, usually in late June. It's a perfect chance to explore hidden gems like the Dean Gardens.

MUST SEE IN YOUR NEIGHBOURHOOD?

The Water of Leith

The Cherry Blossom on Gloucester Street (this is seasonal)

Stockbridge Market

The Black Dinner

Scan here to listen to the audio reading

In 1440, King James II was just 10 years old and a pawn in the power struggles of different factions trying to control Scotland through him. Archibald, the 5th Earl of Douglas, had been in charge until his death but his 16-year-old son didn't have the same authority. With a child ascending to the Earldom and another on the throne, enemies of the powerful Douglas family saw their opportunity.

Sir William Crichton was the new warden of the king and hatched a gruesome plan. He invited the teenage Earl of Douglas and his little brother to dine at Edinburgh Castle with the young James. A feast was held in the great hall of Edinburgh Castle and none of the three boys were aware of what was in store.

During their meal, the head of a black bull was brought in and dropped on the table in front of the Douglas brothers.

It was a sign of treachery and death. There was nothing the 10-year-old king could do but watch in shock as his guests were dragged outside.

A short, sham trial was held where the youngsters were accused of being traitors to the crown. King James is said to have protested on their behalf, but his cries fell on deaf ears and both Douglas boys were beheaded.

While Crichton benefited from what became known as the Black Dinner, there was another figure at work in the background. The brothers' great uncle is believed to have been instrumental in organising the executions and he just happened to be next in line as the 7th Earl of Douglas.

There's infinitely more to Edinburgh's shopping scene than the tourist stores. Scratch beneath the surface and you'll find a world of authentic local goods, designer brands and unique handmade mementoes.

Shops

Kestin

Gift & Lifestyle

From bottles of vintage whisky and local art prints to traditional tweeds and elegant homewares, this is a city that gives you any number of good reasons to part with your cash.

The Red Door Gallery

 Cadenhead's Whisky Shop
235 Old Town

 The Red Door Gallery
236 Old Town

Scotland's oldest independent bottler was founded back in 1842 and has a comfortingly old-fashioned shop on the Royal Mile, where you can taste Scotch whiskies straight from the barrel. Rums, cognacs and gins are also stocked.

This compact contemporary art space on Victoria Street showcases work by more than 150 Scottish and UK artists. Owners Jason and Kathryn curate a selection of fresh and affordable art prints, craft pieces and quirky design products that make great gifts or additions to any home.

 Scan here for more information on each listing. Enter the listing number to see our digital map, images and additional inspiration.

Cadenhead's Whisky Shop

Paper Tiger
Old Town

Established in 1981, this independent retailer stocks a broad range of greetings cards, wrapping paper, gift items and stationery products. With a focus on whimsical and unusual items, you're sure to find something unique to take home or gift to a loved one.

Jeffrey St Whisky & Tobacco
Old Town

An Old Town one-stop shop for whisky, cigars and pipes (and really, what else do you need?), opened by three Edinburgh locals in 2014. It also runs tastings.

Walker Slater
Old Town

Walker Slater makes exceptional suits, jackets and coats from high-quality fabrics such as natural wool and tweed. Colour palettes inspired by Scotland's rugged landscapes lend the garments a distinctive character, while contemporary tailoring ensures they are suitable for a city stroll or a hike in the hills.

Mr Wood's Fossils
Old Town

Mr Wood's Fossils is the place to go for fans of ammonites, trilobites and dinosaur fossils. Suitably situated in the heart of the Old Town, this quirky shop also stocks excellent examples of minerals and meteorites sourced through an international network of trusted suppliers.

Gift & Lifestyle

Lifestory
New Town

Susan Doherty's Scandinavian-led lifestyle store and coffee bar stocks everything you need to give your home a hygge makeover. The carefully curated selection of products ranging from furniture and homewares, to jewellery, stationery and children's toys all display a timeless sense of style.

 St James Quarter
New Town

The St James Quarter provides a vibrant destination for locals and visitors within easy walking distance of Waverley Station. Its wide assortment of high-street and luxury retailers are housed within a day-lit galleria that also contains a multitude of bars and restaurants, as well as a cinema and bowling alley.

 Stòr Lifestyle
New Town

This elegant, ethical lifestyle atelier and bookshop stocks quality handmade goods, homewares, gifts and seasonal flowers on hip Broughton Street. Stòr focuses on artisan-made pieces that are designed to become future heirlooms, along with books and journals that will look great on your coffee table.

 Epitome
New Town

This sleek womenswear emporium on Dundas Street stocks brands such as contemporary Scottish cashmere label Cameron Taylor and German designer Hannoh Wessel.

 Homer
New Town

In a Georgian townhouse on Howe Street, this homeware emporium is split into five carefully curated and themed rooms from the Library to the Kitchen, Bedroom, Shed (for those stylish gardening essentials) and the Living Room where their own range of 'Scot-Scandi' furniture in bespoke Homer Scottish tweed woven in Perthshire is showcased.

 Scottish Design Exchange
New Town

A vibrant hub for local creativity, the Scottish Design Exchange in Edinburgh is a unique retail model that fosters direct connections between artists and buyers. This innovative space in New Town showcases a wide array of Scottish art, fashion, and design, supporting a community of over 150 local artists and designers.

Lifestory

Indie shops not to miss

recommended by @exploringedinburgh

Rosevear Tea
Various Locations

Lifestory
New Town

Pascal & Co
New Town

Topping & Company
New Town

The Pastry Section
Stockbridge

 An Independent Zebra
Stockbridge

This independent Stockbridge retailer stocks a wide range of quirky, colourful and fun items created by local and UK-based makers. You'll find everything from upcycled furniture and handmade jewellery to playful prints celebrating famous Scottish destinations and landmarks.

 The Method
Stockbridge

Brother and sister-act Jodi and Dan Fox set up this minimalist Zen-infused lifestyle store. On the shelves a pared-back selection of incense sticks and candles, cosy alpaca socks and their own luscious skincare brand, made in Scotland, Modm.

 Kestin
Stockbridge

Modern menswear designer Kestin Hare's eponymous flagship store, Kestin, moved from Leith – where his grandfather once ran pubs - to Stockbridge. From the Clyde pant in denim to the Inverness trouser in Gamekeeper Green, the Balloch beanie knitted from local yarn there's more than a nod to Scottish heritage.

I. J. Mellis

I.J. Mellis
Stockbridge

Purveyors of fine farmhouse and artisan cheese for over 30 years, there are three branches of this legendary cheesemonger in Edinburgh (Victoria Street in the Old Town and Morningside as well as Stockbridge). They also offer weekly wine and cheese tastings and pairing events with local producers.

Edinburgh Mercantile
Stockbridge

On North West Circus Place this pared back, artfully curated homeware and gift store pegs itself 'The New Curiosity Shop' and has the vibe of an old general store – but a very contemporary range of must-have objects.

Treen
Stockbridge

Vegan fashion and lifestyle retailer Treen stocks menswear and womenswear that's ethically made and cruelty-free. That's clothing made from organic cotton, linen and hemp to skincare and candles that are kind to the planet and all those who live on it.

Herbie
Stockbridge

This tiny deli on Raeburn Place is a Stockbridge staple. Their chilli jam and homemade marmalade are regular sell-outs and the chicken liver pâté is legendary.

Meander Apparel
Stockbridge

Meander makes versatile, technical clothing for everyday adventures. Designed in Scotland and built to withstand all sorts of weather, the company's garments are inspired by Scandinavian minimalism and are great for compiling a pared-back wardrobe of simple essentials.

Curiouser & Curiouser
New Town & Southside

A treasure trove of design and colour, Curiouser & Curiouser, established by Laura and Ian in 2010, offers a delightful array of illustrative prints, unique jewellery, and stylish homewares.

Rosevear Tea
Various

With no less than three neighbourhood tea shops scattered around the city (the Bruntsfield Place outlet is the original), Rosevear specialises in quality loose-leaf teas and herbal infusions. If you take your cuppa seriously, it's the place to go.

Pascal & Co
Leith

Since opening on Leith Walk in 2021, this arty boutique has become a fulcrum of all things vintage and retro. For an out-of-the-ordinary shopping experience, come and check out its curated, hand-picked selection of pre-loved clothing and other gems.

Bard Scotland
Leith

This gallery and shop in Customs Wharf is dedicated to showcasing the finest craft and design from all over Scotland and the islands and works with around 50 makers. From Laurence Veitch's hand-sculpted and naturally ebonised ash stools to Jonnie Crawford's rippled sycamore bowl to Morven Mulgrew's Weathered Bronzes, each object has a rich story.

TBCo
Leith

TBCo designs and produces natural, sustainable and beautiful textiles including its signature tartan blankets. Its store on Great Junction Street gives shoppers a chance to experience the soft and cosy feel of its blankets, scarves, pyjamas and accessories, many of which are made using recycled wool.

Valvona & Crolla
Leith Walk

The original Edinburgh deli and Italian wine merchant, founded in 1934, this gourmand's stalwart on Elm Row is an Aladdin's cave with hams hanging from the ceiling and shelves brimming with jars of artisan honey.

Tommy
Saorsa Art Gallery

West End

See page 73 for more information on Saorsa Art Gallery.

What is your favourite thing about Stockbridge?

My favourite thing about Stockbridge is the 'village' type atmosphere it has, from the wee independent shops, bakers, cafés to the mix of people that make it what it is. The architecture of the buildings in Stockbridge is beautiful also making it a wonderful place to be.

Where in Edinburgh do you find the most inspiration for your work?

I am originally from Dundee and Arran so I love being near the sea, so I travel a lot around Newhaven and Portobello with the dogs and I'm always inspired by this. Stockbridge has The Waters of Leith running through it and this is a real bonus to me.

MUST SEE IN YOUR NEIGHBOURHOOD?

The Water of Leith Walkway

Inverleith Park

Royal Botanic Garden

Armchair Books

Bookshops

As you might expect from somewhere that was named the first ever UNESCO City of Literature in 2004, Edinburgh knows plenty about the pleasures of a good bookshop.

Armchair Books

Armchair Books
Old Town

Situated on Edinburgh's historic West Port, Armchair Books is an intimate and authentic family-run store stocking an exceptional selection of secondhand books. Browse its crowded shelves for hidden gems or ask the knowledgeable staff to help you source something special.

Blackwell's Bookshop
Old Town

This national bookseller has a history dating back to the mid-19th century. Its Edinburgh store opened in 2002 opposite the University of Edinburgh's Old College on South Bridge and is popular with students shopping for term-time textbooks. It also stocks a selection of gifts, games and stationery.

Topping & Company
New Town

This family-run independent bookseller has shops in Bath, Ely and St Andrews, as well as this beautiful store on Blenheim Place, which opened in 2021. The shop's year-round Literary Festival offers a chance to see award-winning authors and celebrities discuss their latest books.

Typewronger Books
New Town

Where words meet clatter, discover Typewronger Books - Edinburgh's tiniest bookshop and Scotland's exclusive typewriter repair hub. Fostering a vibrant community of artists, musicians and bibliophiles, independent publications and zines share space with new books and the rhythmic symphony of typewriters.

McNaughtan's
New Town

Established in 1957, McNaughtan's is the oldest second-hand and antiquarian bookshop in Scotland. Expect to find rare and collectable editions of great literary works. Part of the basement premises now houses Typewronger Books – Edinburgh's smallest bookshop and Scotland's only typewriter repair shop.

Scan here for more information on each listing. Enter the listing number to see our digital map, images and additional inspiration.

Bookshops

Free Library Movement

266 — 17 Dundas Street
New Town

It might be bright red, but tucked away down a few steps off Dundas Street, you might walk right past this Little Free Library. Set up by short-term let company Dickins, it's perfect for picking up a read on your way into the city centre.

267 — Teviotdale Place
Stockbridge

Edinburgh's first Little Free Library was established by book artist Rachel Hazell in the Stockbridge Colonies. With a rustic wooden frame and glass front beckoning readers to "take a book, leave a book", it's as quaint as the homes that surround it.

268 — 61 Comely Bank Road
Stockbridge

One of the brighter designs of Edinburgh's Little Free Libraries can be found in Comely Bank. With a pitched roof and carved decorations, you can't miss this wee book-filled house.

269 — The Gently Mad Book Shop
Stockbridge

A short wander from the Royal Botanic Garden you'll find this traditional bookshop, which has an enjoyable stuck-in-time ambiance and doubles as a bookbinder. If you like the smell of dusty old books, you'll love it.

270 — Golden Hare Books
Stockbridge

Situated in the heart of Stockbridge, Golden Hare Books is a charming independent bookseller stocking a carefully curated selection of the latest fiction and non-fiction titles. The books are beautifully displayed in a welcoming space with a log fire that makes it hard to leave on chillier days.

Scan here for more information on each listing. Enter the listing number to see our digital map, images and additional inspiration.

Golden Hare Books

Tills Bookshop

The Portobello Bookshop

 Tills Bookshop
271 Southside

 The Portobello Bookshop
272 Portobello

Established in 1985, Tills is one of Edinburgh's oldest second-hand bookshops. Pick up a rare first edition or peruse shelves packed with a large selection of fiction and non-fiction books. There's a fireplace, some places to perch and knowledgable staff on hand for some bookish banter.

Head to Porty to browse a diverse range of fiction, non-fiction and children's titles in this welcoming and well-stocked independent bookseller. The shop opened in 2019 and has since become a mainstay of the local literary community, hosting regular events and book signings

Scan here for more information on each listing. Enter the listing number to see our digital map, images and additional inspiration.

Kathryn

Red Door Gallery

Old Town

See page 138 for more information on Red Door Gallery.

Being located on one of the busiest streets in Edinburgh, where would you recommend going to escape the hustle and bustle?

When the sun is shining, head to 'The Meadows', or visit the National Museum of Scotland for some quiet reflection, or head to Stockbridge for shops and cafés (there is a market on Sunday).

When looking for a souvenir to take home from Edinburgh what would you say is the ideal gift?

Well what can I say, an Art Print from The Red Door Gallery is the perfect souvenir to create 'that special memory' from your Edinburgh visit. We may be a small space but with over 100 artists to choose from we have something for everyone!

MUST SEE IN YOUR NEIGHBOURHOOD?

The Vennel Steps

Mary's Milk Bar

St Giles' Cathedral

The Salt Horse for beer

The Bow Bar for whisky

Johnny
One-Arm

Scan here to listen
to the audio reading

*In the 17th century, an Edinburgh man
called John Chiesley was ordered by the
courts to pay a huge sum of money in
child maintenance. John wasn't happy
about the decision, and like many
disgruntled citizens, spat threats at the
judge. This was all part of the job for Sir
George Lockhart though. He was used to
being threatened daily.*

A few months later, George was
attending a service in St Giles' Kirk,
having completely forgotten about the
incident with Chiesley. As he walked out
of the church, a vaguely familiar character
greeted the judge and he nodded his head
in return.

It wasn't far to George's Edinburgh
residence, but he had the strange feeling
that somebody was behind him. This
was a stout member of Edinburgh's high
society though: he didn't scare easily.
He did however start to pick up the
pace. As George turned and approached
his home, there was no doubt that he was
being followed.

As he fumbled for his keys, a voice called
out behind him. Turning around, George
was met with the barrel of a pistol and
the grinning face of John Chiesley.
Without any subtlety, John shot the judge,
bragging to the world that he had carried
out his own justice.

It was a short trial and for murdering
such an influential figure, John was
tortured before his execution. His legs
were broken, the arm he fired the pistol
with was chopped off and he was hanged.
The murderer was supposed to be kept on
display as a warning, but after a few days,
the body vanished.

Soon, reports of ghostly, shuffling footsteps
following people down the Edinburgh
streets began. Rumours of a one-armed
man lurking in the dark spread around the
city. Eventually, in 1965 during some house
renovations in Dalry, a skeleton with only
one arm and a rusty pistol hanging around
its neck was found. It could be none other
than Johnny One Arm.

The skeleton was laid to rest and the
ghost sightings suddenly stopped. The
missing arm has never been found though,
so while most of John Chiesley is able to
rest, there might be one part still dragging
itself around the cobbles of Edinburgh.

The popularity of Edinburgh as a visitor
destination means you'll find accommodation
to suit all tastes. Big-brand hotels share
the map with boutique properties and
luxury boltholes and laid-back B&Bs.
One tip: book well ahead of time if you can.

Accommodation

The Balmoral

Porteous' Studio

The Scotsman

 273 **Porteous' Studio**
Old Town

 274 **The Scotsman**
Old Town

There's a huge amount to love about this two-person self-catering retreat in the Old Town. The studio was originally garage space when it was purchased by a local couple in 2016, but has subsequently been lovingly renovated with natural materials, introducing an open kitchen, a double bed and underfloor heating.

Named for the national newspaper that previously occupied these Baroque buildings on North Bridge, The Scotsman is now a luxury hotel that retains many original features. If the stunning views of Edinburgh's skyline aren't enough, there's an intimate cinema in the basement showing a curated film programme.

 Scan here for more information on each listing. Enter the listing number to see our digital map, images and additional inspiration.

Market Street Hotel

Kick Ass Hostels

The Witchery

Market Street Hotel
Old Town

Market Street Hotel is a bold and contemporary addition to the historic skyline of Edinburgh's Old Town. Scotland's first member of the global Design Hotels collection is notable for its stylish Scandi-Scot interiors. The top-floor lounge and champagne bar provide a spectacular view of the city's iconic landmarks.

Virgin Hotels Edinburgh
Old Town

This newly opened hotel housed in a cluster of renovated historic buildings in the heart of the Old Town contains 222 smartly designed guest rooms and suites. There are also multiple dining and drinking destinations including Eve – an all-day venue for food and drinks with regular live entertainment.

The Witchery
Old Town

There's nowhere in Scotland quite like The Witchery. Housed in buildings that date back to the 17th century, its nine unique suites are decadently decorated in a gothic style. Perfect for a romantic stay, you can also enjoy a meal in the candlelit fine-dining restaurant.

House of Gods
Old Town

"Unapologetic extravagance" is how the House of Gods hotel describes its unique approach to style and service. Rooms range in size from the compact Orient Express-inspired Cabin to grand suites featuring a bespoke cocktail bar. Available upgrades include an on-call butler service and luxury breakfast hamper.

Kick Ass Hostels
Old Town

The name says plenty. 'High quality, affordable and fun' runs the tagline of this popular hostel chain, which has two centrally located Edinburgh properties – one in Grassmarket, the other in Greyfriars. Both have bars on site and are open to over-18s only.

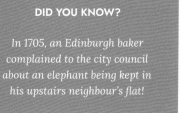

DID YOU KNOW?

In 1705, an Edinburgh baker complained to the city council about an elephant being kept in his upstairs neighbour's flat!

The Balmoral

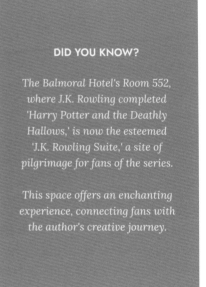

DID YOU KNOW?

The Balmoral Hotel's Room 552, where J.K. Rowling completed 'Harry Potter and the Deathly Hallows,' is now the esteemed 'J.K. Rowling Suite,' a site of pilgrimage for fans of the series.

This space offers an enchanting experience, connecting fans with the author's creative journey.

280 CoDE Pod Hostels: THE CoURT
Old Town

A Japanese pod-style hostel in the Old Town, based in a former courthouse and jail. There are private rooms as well as pod dorms, and breakfast is on offer too. The same brand also offers THE LoFT, a co-living space aimed at long-term travellers.

281 Cheval Old Town Chambers
Old Town

Locations don't come much more prime than the one enjoyed by the Cheval Old Town Chambers, which offers more than 70 stylish apartments on the Royal Mile, virtually in the shadow of St Giles' Cathedral. The apartments themselves range in size from studios to penthouses.

Scan here for more information on each listing. Enter the listing number to see our digital map, images and additional inspiration.

The Balmoral
New Town

Edinburgh's most iconic hotel, The Balmoral rises majestically above Waverley Station at the east end of Princes Street. Its stylish rooms and suites offer all the luxuries you would expect from five-star accommodation, while its Number One restaurant holds a coveted Michelin star.

Waldorf Astoria - The Caledonian
New Town

Another of Edinburgh's grand Victorian railway hotels, the building nicknamed "The Caley" has stood at the west end of Princes Street since 1903. Now operated by the Waldorf Astoria brand, the five-star hotel contains a luxury Guerlain spa, several dining areas and a lounge housed in the original station concourse.

Gleneagles Townhouse
New Town

This urban outpost of the famed Gleneagles Hotel in Perthshire occupies a former bank building on the east side of St Andrew Square. Alongside its handsome boutique bedrooms, the Townhouse contains a members' club, an all-day restaurant and a rooftop bar accessible to hotel guests.

24 Royal Terrace
New Town

This family-run boutique hotel situated in a grand Georgian townhouse at the foot of Calton Hill stands out thanks to its impressive display of contemporary artworks. Pieces from owner Alan Campbell's private collection adorn the bedrooms and public areas including a secretive late-night bar.

Cheval The Edinburgh Grand
New Town

Cheval The Edinburgh Grand offers high-spec self-catering accommodation housed in another of Edinburgh's former banks. The apartments range from studios to three-bedroom spaces, all with their own kitchen and living area. The penthouse has stunning views over the city towards Arthur's Seat.

Kimpton Charlotte Square
New Town

Spread across seven interconnected Georgian townhouses in the heart of the New Town, Kimpton Charlotte Square blends classical elegance with modern vibes. The hotel's luxury spa offers a range of specialty treatments, while guests can enjoy high-end modern cuisine at Aizle or Mediterranean mezze flavours at BABA.

Accommodation

Observatory House

Eden Locke
New Town

Based on George Street, in Edinburgh's New Town, these renovated Georgian buildings contain no less than 72 apartments. Among other features on the premises, you'll also find a coffee shop and co-working space. It's dog-friendly, too, which should get tails wagging.

The Baxter Hostel
New Town

Billed as a boutique hostel, and sitting in an old members' club close to Princes Street in the New Town, The Baxter offers classily designed dorms, including a four-bed private hire room. Two dorms are female-only, and there's also an attractive lounge area on site, complete with free tea and coffee.

Rockhouse
New Town

Sitting at the foot of Calton Hill, and said to be one of the earliest properties built in the New Town, this 17th-century merchant's house has been reinvented as a trio of impressive self-catering properties. The main house sleeps eight, and there's also a smaller terrace apartment and studio.

Observatory House
New Town

After a room with a view? You won't do better than this remarkable period building set high on Calton Hill, with city panoramas on all sides. Formerly a stargazing observatory and now a contemporary art hub, it has two self-catering properties, sleeping four and two respectively.

Nine Nelson
New Town

This beautifully appointed Georgian apartment in the New Town – located at, yes, No. 9 Nelson Street – can sleep up to nine, making it a brilliant option for larger groups. Features include a grand staircase, flagstone floors, designer furniture and a huge amount of natural light.

Native
New Town

This slick operation offers crisply decorated, fully serviced apartments in the New Town, close to all the key sights – breakfast in a bag is offered with all rates. On site, you'll also find a venue called The Counter, which offers lunch, cocktails and a range of cultural events.

Accommodation

The Raeburn
Stockbridge

The Raeburn is a luxury boutique hotel housed in an impressive detached Georgian property at the end of Stockbridge's hip high street. Its bar and restaurant are popular with locals, especially in the summer months when punters spill out onto the large terrace.

Canon Cave
Stockbridge

An upmarket basement hideaway close to the Royal Botanic Gardens, this self-catering gem combines the funky and the traditional – you'll find underfloor heating, a super kingsize bed and a Sonos soundbar alongside a wood-burning stove, copper bath tub and original stonework.

Prestonfield House
Southside

With a stunning setting at the base of Arthur's Seat, this 17th-century manor house is now a luxurious five-star hotel with 18 bedrooms and five romantic suites. The opulent and theatrically decorated public rooms include the Baroque Tapestry Room, which provides a sumptuous backdrop for a decadent afternoon tea.

Dovecot Cottage
West End

This remarkable building was once home to pigeons, as its name suggests, but has been converted into a gloriously atmospheric holiday cottage, about fifteen minutes on foot from the Old Town. Expect bare stone walls, a cedarwood kitchen, garden views and a three-person bedroom set in a tower.

Murrayfield Hotel
West End

This stylish hotel is the ideal place to stay if attending one of the many sporting events or concerts that take place throughout the year at nearby Murrayfield Stadium. The hotel is within easy reach of the city centre and has an on-site restaurant serving classic Scottish dishes.

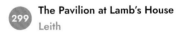

The Pavilion at Lamb's House
Leith

This classy little self-catering property is split over three floors, with a double or twin bedroom on each. Touches of luxury and plenty of antique furnishings make it a great proposition for a memorable stay – and it's located right on The Shore in the heart of Leith.

Prestonfield House

Fingal

Fingal
Leith

When it was first launched in 1963, Fingal was a Northern Lighthouse vessel, ferrying lighthouse keepers, essential supplies and maintenance staff to lighthouses, as well as undertaking repairs to navigational aids. How times have changed. Today the ship has become a luxury floating hotel, moored 10 minutes away from sister ship The Royal Yacht Britannia and boasting not only the AA Hotel of the Year Scotland 2023-24 and an AA five-star rating for its accommodation, but also two AA rosettes for its dining.

There are 22 cabins, including several duplex rooms and the Skerryvore Suite, which comes with a private deck area. The Lighthouse Restaurant and Bar specialises in fine dining (its salmon is smoked on board) and also does an indulgent afternoon tea.

Cat
Treen

Stockbridge

See page 143 for more information on Treen.

Other than Treen, where else would you recommend shopping in Edinburgh?

If I had one day, I'd head to The Method for wellness and skincare, 5th Season Vintage for the best pre-loved picks, ALC for daywear, and Catalog for interiors, rounded off with a cocktail at The Last Word.

And where would you recommend stopping for a bite to eat to recharge?

Florentines for a sausage butty, Bell's Diner for the best burger in town, Cheese n' Toasted for exactly that, Cowan & Sons for coffee and cake or Smith & Gertrude for wine and snacks if that's the kind of day you're having.

MUST SEE IN YOUR NEIGHBOURHOOD?

Royal Botanic Garden

The Stockbridge Arch

Inverleith Park

Dean Village

Circus Lane

Greyfriars Bobby

Scan here to listen to the audio reading

The story of Greyfriars Bobby is one of the most loved from Edinburgh's long history. It's a heartwarming tale of the most faithful dog in the world.

Bobby was a Skye Terrier that belonged to a local night watchman called John Gray. The pair were inseparable, and the wee dog kept his owner company through all kinds of weather while patrolling the city streets. Even after old John died in 1856 and was buried in Greyfriars Kirkyard, that close bond continued.

Legend says that Bobby lay down on the grass and refused to leave his master's grave. No matter how many times he was chased out by the caretaker, the faithful dog sneaked back in to take up his post. As the story of Greyfriars Bobby spread, the terrier became a local celebrity.

Crowds began to gather every day to see Bobby, and when the one o'clock Gun fired from Edinburgh Castle, he would trot round to a nearby coffee house for lunch. One tradition states this was where he ate with John before his death, while another claims the owner trained the dog to listen out for the gun since it was so good for business!

A new law could have been the end of Greyfriars Bobby when all dogs in Edinburgh were required to be licensed by an owner or destroyed. The Lord Provost himself took care of the paperwork and presented the dog with a collar in 1867.

Bobby remained by his master's grave for 14 years, well cared for by the people of Edinburgh, until his own time was up. He was buried nearby and even has his own gravestone at the entrance to Greyfriars Kirkyard inscribed with: "Let his loyalty and devotion be a lesson to us all."

Shortly after Bobby died, Lady Burdett-Coutts paid to have the famous drinking fountain built outside the graveyard. It's become a popular attraction for those who are moved by the story, although the rubbing of Bobby's nose is inadvertently destroying the monument. Much better just to admire his likeness and ensure it's around for many more generations to be inspired by the most faithful dog in the world.

One of Edinburgh's biggest assets is the wealth of different destinations and activities on its outskirts – here are the best of them.

Day Trips

Jupiter Artland

The Forth Bridge

Edinburgh's position on the national map – with the green contours of the Lothian countryside ringing the city on three sides and the Firth of Forth flowing away to its north – makes it ideally placed for out-of-town excursions. The region as a whole is a fascinating one, and the combination of short distances and good rail and bus links means day-trips are easy to arrange.

The options we've included here all add a slightly different flavour to an Edinburgh trip, bringing more context to the region where today's capital city grew and evolved. In several cases, they can also give you a chance to recharge away from some of the busier city centre attractions.

Scan here for more information on each listing. Enter the listing number to see our digital map, images and additional inspiration.

PENTLAND HILLS

NORTH BERWICK

The handsome rumple of green slopes to the southwest of the city are known as the Pentland Hills. They stretch for some 20 miles from end to end, providing ample opportunity for a proper dose of the outdoors. One popular walking trail is the 6.5-mile Pentland Five Peaks, which snakes over the summits of West Kip, East Kip, Scald Law, Carnethy Hill and Turnhouse Hill. The start and end points (Nine Mile Burn and Flotterstone) are both close to bus stops.

Perched on a headland overlooking the estuary, the coastal town of North Berwick is easily reached by either bus or train from central Edinburgh. Expect the usual seaside perks, from fish and chip shops to beachfront ice cream parlours, as well as great golf courses and the five-star Scottish Seabird Centre. Bass Rock, a couple of miles offshore, is home to a vast colony of gannets throughout the spring and summer.

PORTOBELLO

SOUTH QUEENSFERRY

Edinburgh's very own seaside suburb sits just three miles east of the city centre and has a long history covering everything from gangs of smugglers to Victorian pleasure-seekers. Today, a broad sandy beach and grand Georgian terraces still give off an air of its old-time grandeur. Seek out the enjoyable Tanifiki Café for a pit stop.

Where the three Forth Bridges stretch out across the water – some eight miles west of the city – you'll find South Queensferry, a historic village that retains a certain kooky charm. The bridges are an attraction in their own right, particularly the oldest and most famous of the trio, which is now UNESCO-listed. Hopetoun House, an opulent stately home on the village outskirts, is well worth a visit.

Castles near Edinburgh

recommended by David C. Weinczok

Craigmillar Castle
Southeast Edinburgh

Blackness Castle
Blackness

Tantallon Castle
East Lothian

Aberdour Castle
Aberdour

Stirling Castle
Stirling

Linlithgow Palace
Linlithgow

In the 15th and 16th centuries, these hulking ruins were a sumptuous residence for the monarchs of Scotland – Mary Queen of Scots was actually born here – but after a fire in 1746, they're now a visitor attraction.

Jupiter Artland
Wilkieston

A superb contemporary sculpture park to the west of the city, with site-specific works created by Anish Kapoor, Antony Gormley and many more.

Colinton Tunnel
Colinton

The last train ran through this Victorian rail tunnel in 1967. Since then it's been reinvented as a public walkway, decorated within by Scotland's largest mural.

Inchcolm Island
Firth of Forth

Join Forth Boat Tours for the chance to visit this fascinating little island in the Firth of Forth, where a medieval abbey shares space with a WWII coastal battery and all manner of different seabirds.

Bass Rock Tour

Rosslyn Chapel

 Bass Rock Tour
305 North Berwick

 Rosslyn Chapel
306 Roslin

Here's a 90-minute tour you won't forget in a hurry. Sula Boat Trips sails out from North Berwick during the spring and summer breeding season to reach Bass Rock, home to the largest colony of North Atlantic gannets on the planet.

When Dan Brown's best-selling novel The Da Vinci Code included the claim that the Holy Grail was buried at Rosslyn Chapel, it brought fresh fame to this ornate 15th-century place of worship. It sits in the former mining village of Roslin, directly south of Edinburgh and connected to the city by bus.

Scan here for more information on each listing. Enter the listing number to see our digital map, images and additional inspiration.

WITH THANKS TO OUR PARTNERS

Hidden Scotland

Milton of Crathes

Banchory

AB31 5QH

SCOTLAND

Text © 2024 by Hidden Scotland.

All rights reserved.

Printed in the United Kingdom

First Edition - February 2024

ISBN 978-1-3999-6828-7

AUTHORS

Ben Lerwill

Lucy Gillmore

Graeme Johncock

Alyn Griffiths

David C. Weinczok

Jack Cairney

Shawna Law

ILLUSTRATIONS

Joe Mclaren

DESIGN

Karla Hall

Siobhan Ogg

PHOTOGRAPHY

Simon Hird